I0751032

ALSO BY SANDRA GORE NIELSEN

"A True Love Story." *Life Choices - Navigating Difficult Paths,* an anthology published by Turning Point International.

www.sandraoffthestrip.com, an online magazine blog dedicated to the adventures of an eclectic mind.

Author Online
For updates and more resources
www.SandraGoreNielsen.com

The Black & White

Sex and the Zen of Shopping

Live Rich by Shopping Smart

Be fabulously frugal
with bargains and deals in
clothing , jewelry and home furnishings
- new, vintage, and secondhand.

created by

Sandra Gore Nielsen

ISBN 978-0-9842799-1-3

Library of Congress Control Number: 2009940673

Tajine Publishing, Inc.
2550 E Desert Inn Rd #443
Las Vegas NV 89121-3611

Wholesale Distribution:
Lightning Source and distribution partners Ingram, Amazon.com,
Baker & Taylor, Barnes & Noble, Nacscorp and Espresso Book Machine
Retail Orders:
Amazon.com, other Online Retailers and Bookstores

First Black and White Edition. Version 3.0

DISCLAIMER

The purpose of this book is to educate and entertain. The opinions expressed are the author's and not intended to be final authority on any issue. The material contained herein is not intended to be all inclusive. Any companies, stores or labels mentioned are not specifically endorsed and the author is not receiving any compensation for their inclusion in the book. The shopping results achieved by the author are not guaranteed in any way. All savings using the methods described in the book are subject to circumstance and individual effort and not guaranteed in any way. Neither the author nor publisher are responsible for the behavior of any individual who claims influence by any methodology or philososphy described in the book. Every effort has been made to make this manual as complete and accurate as possible, but not guaranteeed. It contains information that is current only up to the time of writing.

Shopping is to women what sex is to men. They can never get enough.

Thank you to my shopping mentor, Esperanza, who inspired me to codify the adventures of our Saturday morning antiquing expeditions.

And as always, thank you to my dear husband who supports me in all things and pushed me to "finish the book!"

A Peek in the Attic
Old Mission School Thrift Store
'vintage clothing and more'

Table of contents

Sandra Gore Nielsen

Victor Costa top - $25 - antique mall
BCBG leather pants - $11 - antique mall
Nine West knee-high python boots - $30 - Macy's
Chinese vases - $10 ea - estate sale
19th c. Swedish oil painting w/ gold leaf frame - inherited

Preface

why this book and why me?

When 89% of women surveyed say they'd rather go shopping alone than with their husbands, and half say they'd rather go shopping than ***be*** with their men[1], can there be any doubt about the depth of our passion? We aren't talking optional behavior patterns. Shopping to women is about basic needs and instinct, as strong a drive as sex is to men.

What's Zen got to do with it? With Zen (correct mindset), all things are possible. Without it, very little is - certainly not satisfaction or happiness. Shop Zen and you step out in style from head to toe for less than $70. You can furnish a 1000 ft^2 condo for under $2500. Shop Zen and you can live rich on any budget. I did it and so can you. It's all in the book.

I created Sex Zen and Shopping for women who like to shop and for men who might not understand why. I want you to keep shopping no matter your budget because shopping is fun and you deserve it. You just need the tools to do it responsibly. It won't feel like a sacrifice, I promise.

My goal is simple. I want you to have more beauty and pleasure in life and to be more adventurous and daring. I want you to be more *free.*

Relax. Let go. Have fun. Look good. Live rich.
Let the Universe take you for a happy ride.

Female torso - $17 - antique mall
3-tiered candelabra - $2 - Goodwill
Green glass decanter - $12 - antique shop
Golden candlestick - $3 - Salvation Army
Fireplace with heater - $275 - Big Lots
Black and yellow ceramic pot - $20 - garage sale
Zebra rug - $100 - closeout sale
19th c French oil painting w/gold leaf frame - inherited

shop zen!
what's money got to do with it?

Money is unbearably tight and life is too sober. What's a girl to do when she needs some release from the drudgery? You can always go shopping. The thrill of the kill is intoxicating. Your juices flow, your pulse races. You are powerful. You feel good.

You're thinking, *"That's pretty irresponsible - telling me to shop when I need my money to pay bills."* Or, *"I'm trying to save every penny. I can't allow myself anything frivolous."* It is true you can't *spend* like you used to, but that doesn't mean you can't *shop*. Of course, money is important. But more important than the *amount* of money is *how* you use it – your shopping habits. Are they dumb or smart?

Shopping is to women what sex is to men.

Why *does* shopping make you feel better? It's simple. You are a woman; women are genetically engineered to feather their nests and adorn their bodies. It is the Nature of Things. The female appetite for shopping is no different from the male craving for sex. Law of Nature: shopping is to women what sex is to men; they can never get enough.

Rich or poor, all women love to shop.

The euphoria of shopping with its titillating pleasures is the same for women everywhere, rich or poor - and from the very beginning of time. Our ancestors started adorning their bodies and collecting precious trinkets the moment they first started walking upright. Any archaeologist will tell you the earliest graves of mankind yield three things: bones, pots and **beads.**

DID YOU KNOW?

74% of surveyed British females think about shopping every 60 seconds while men think of sex every 52 seconds[2].

You might think that declaring shopping celibacy is the righteous path for you and your budget, but it's just not realistic. Denial of such a basic passion leads to frustration, and frustration leads to unhappiness, irritation and wild mood swings. It can't be sustained in the long term without dire emotional cost - and risk of binging. Allow yourself to indulge a most natural instinct, but do it in ways that are fun and cheap. You can be fabulously frugal while having sublime adventures. Really.

Relax. Beautiful clothes and objects are out there for very little money. You can find them and have fun doing it. The first step is the hardest - you must free yourself from the *bourgeois* baggage you've been lugging around most of your life. Forget about who spends the most on a designer bag and from what overpriced store. Bragging rights today go to those who pay the least.

Bragging rights go to those who pay the least.

Smart ladies, with money to buy everything, still *love* to get a deal, and *love more* to tell you about it. Shopping is a game Sylvia plays for her own pleasure. She's long past needing anything for herself, her daughters, or grandchildren. But she *craves* the blood rush thrill of the hunt. Sylvia solved her problem by becoming a 'philanthropic shopper' - she shops for charity. "*You can be a minimalist and shop every day,*" she says, "*as long as you give it all away.*" She's drawn to the baby department by a sign offering 75% off. No infants in her family, she's not so much interested in what she's buying as in the percentage off: the killer deal. There are needy Baby Doe's in all sizes, so she just has fun buying. Her eyes sparkle, her heart races - all in a good cause; good for everyone - for Sylvia, for the store, for the lucky recipients of the bounty of her ardent passion to shop.

Don't despair if you're struggling just to take care of yourself – or your family. You can get exactly the same thrill as Sylvia. It's not important *how much* you spend, but *how exciting* the hunt and the kill. Imagine a glorious Versace gown you unearth in a hidden, dusty, overstuffed shop – one that cost you pennies on the dollar. If you look and feel like a diva, who cares where it came from, who owned it, or what it cost? Buy things cheap and give them to your friends. You'll feel great and they will too.

This is really easy. You can do it. Who's conflicted over buying pre-owned real estate, art or cars? Everyone's impressed with a beautifully restored ante-bellum manor. The more detailed the *provenance* of an oil painting, the more value it has at Christie's. Who asks how much you paid for your BMW — or if it was brand new when you drove it off the lot? You get the wow power without paying the full ticket - plus you help the environment by recycling. Pamper yourself while being socially responsible.

Pamper yourself while being socially responsible.

You *can* change your life by changing your attitude toward shopping. The life skills needed to succeed at Zen shopping are exactly those you need to live a rich life - a fun life - a happy life.

Shopping Sisters
Nancy and Barb
Children's Cabinet Thrift Store
Incline Village, Lake Tahoe

Step 1
break old habits

It's time to get over yourself, develop a new world view, and let go of old ideas about self-worth being measured by what you own and how much it cost. You are not the object - nor are you the price of the object. You own it - it doesn't own you. It exists for your pleasure. Did you buy something beautiful for the cost of a martini? Applaud your resourcefulness and good fortune. Don't feel you are less; feel you are more.

Don't feel you are less.
Feel you are more.

Everything you need is encoded in the survival genes of your DNA. Portrayed as gatherers on the lookout for the sweetest and choicest berries, the real story is that cavewomen were also hunters. Female adrenalin pumped as hard as any male in the ecstasy of the kill.

Be you

Retailers skillfully guide us to the purchases they want us to make. Not much imagination or creativity needed in a ladies department with this season's colors and styles carefully sorted by size into rows of identical dresses or piles of designer jeans neatly stacked on tabletops according to waist measurement. It's all been laid out for effortless and unchallenging selection. The retailers have chosen for you, and you are not only allowing them to mold you, you are paying them to do it.

Activate your right brain and get in touch with your instincts.

You *do* have to make some extra effort, to think out of the box. To save money and get the best deals, you must look where sizes, colors and styles are *not* laid out in an appealing display. Activate your right brain, give your intuition free rein, and get in touch with your instincts. It's not really work; it's a quest for a unique new you - an adventure that opens doors to heady experiences, fascinating people and amazing treasures.

Candlesticks - $2 to $3 each Goodwill

Step 2
it's all up to you

There are three laws that govern the universe of shopping — very simple and easy to master.

law #1: **"$$$ = order."** The pricier the boutique, the more carefully the few items are displayed. When you enter a white-walled, parquet-floored designer shop stocked with a dozen different selections in teeny-weeny sizes very artfully arranged, you know the price tag is going to be inversely proportionate to the number of dresses. If you don't have big bucks and a skinny *tush*, you're in the wrong place.

law #2: If "$$$ = order," then **"cheap = chaos."** The cheaper the price and the bigger the mess, the more likely you are to find a bargain. Discount stores like Marshalls save costs on overhead and pass on those savings to you. You dig deep through the long, overloaded racks. You quickly finger your way through the packed hangers of cheesy tops to find a BCBG beaded sweater that retailed for $150 (*crazy!*) and is here priced $39.95. Let the uninitiated turn up their noses at 'rack-shopping' while you pick out the best bits.

law #3: **"The bigger the bargain, the more you hunt."** Okay, you *do* work a little harder to earn those savings. Think of a retail store price as containing a finder's fee; the time and energy spent in the hunt earns you that fee. You accept this challenge if you want to look great, but don't have the money to shop in ways you think you deserve. You sacrifice ease for affordability, but without sacrificing quality. It's a more than fair trade off when your bank account is shrinking.

law #1 $$$ = order
law #2 cheap = chaos
law #3 The bigger the bargain,
the more you hunt.

At the other end of the spectrum from a Georgio Armani '*$$$ = order*' boutique is the swap meet with jumbles of clothing strewn on shower curtains on the ground. No attempt at order here. No clarity provided. This is the ultimate hunting ground for the serious bargain shopper.

A swap meet is quintessential '*cheap = chaos.*' With a carefully trained eye and a no-shame willingness to dig deep, a random pile of castoffs gives up an aquamarine Chinese embroidered silk robe for $3. No stains, no loose seams and a perfect fit. It doesn't get better than this.

Chinese robe
– $3
swap meet

Second thoughts about wearing an Oriental treasure because you don't know who had it on last, what they did — or where it came from? Get over it. Be thrilled with the prize catch of the day. Relish your elegant look; enjoy your bragging rights; savor the respect from your friends when you tell them how much (little) you paid – *if* you choose to do so. You are the triumphant huntress flaunting your trophy; you satisfied a primal urge and it cost you $3.

to tell or not to tell—it's up to you

It is *totally* okay if you're not comfortable revealing how little you paid or where you shop. You make the rules. It's your choice if you want to be admired for your sumptuous finds and let everyone think you're paying full price. Moral standards? Forget about little white lies. You're in the wild west of shopping with no disclosure policies. You might be proud to share the details of your latest conquest – or not. It *is* hard though to resist gloating a bit over a particularly killer deal. You long to share.

Ostrich boa
Reversible with long plumes on one side and short on the other.
- $50 - antique mall

You quickly discover who in your circle has moved beyond hang-ups about *where* things come from and into appreciating *how sexy* it is to find something so wonderful for so cheap. You feel powerful - in charge. Showcase your spoils. Everything you buy has a story; you are the conqueror with riveting tales to tell.

Everything you buy has a story.

Let those who haven't made the attitude shift think what they will. Accept their compliments with "*Thank you, I do so love Chanel,*" and give them your best Mona Lisa smile. The real price and the real story are yours to share in triumph - or hold in secret, whichever suits your fancy.

Step 3
get a killer deal

Get the best price on everything that you buy. This is how you stretch a tight budget and continue shopping far longer than you otherwise could afford. The less you pay for one thing, the more you have to spend on something else. The only time you want to relent on price is when compassion calls for you to be fair and humane and not take advantage of someone in sad circumstances - sadder than yours. I call it *doing business with a conscience.*

The less you pay for one thing, the more you have to spend on something else.

The typical American pays the price marked on the tag. If you're not yet comfortable with bargaining, at the very least, you must look for tags with price reductions. Never pay full price for anything. There are too many stores discounting merchandise to buy anything that isn't on sale.

Good if the price tag is reduced, but better still if you are promised additional discounts at the register. Keep track of those extra discounts. Do the math. Question the price. If the clerk makes a mistake, correct her. Fight for every penny. There is no shame here, only your loss if you don't take advantage of every opportunity to save so that you can spend more.

Never pay full price for anything.

Sylvia is a smart lady, a single mom who built a real estate empire. She understands money and instructs her grandkids by taking them on shopping safaris at Macy's when she gets "extra-20% off" coupons. She gives each a $40 budget and an hour to shop the store.

Whoever scores the biggest %$ savings gets a $20 prize. While they're scouring the store for the best deals, they're learning math and what the discount signs really mean in terms of savings. *Example:* $30 blouse marked "*65% off*": Subtract 65% from 100% to get 35%. Take 35% of $30 to get $11 (approx). If you have an additional 20% off, the final price is $11 minus $2+ (20% of 11) or less than $9!

DID YOU KNOW?

50% off with an extra 50% off = 75% off.

Don't be intimidated. Never be afraid to ask for a better price. It might seem awkward at the local mall, but you *can* do it and you might get that discount just because you asked – usually when the merchandise is damaged in some way. Ask for a percentage off for a small stain, scratch, or even a loose button. The clerk will check with her manager, who may see that the item is destined for the sale table eventually, and give you the discount now.

Going out of business
- 25% discount is just the starting point.
antique mall

A consignment shop usually won't discount until an item has been in stock for an agreed-upon period of time. But when that time elapses, both the owner and the shop are ready to see it move and always open to an offer. It's pretty much always the same story. A pricey Ellen Tracy suit in perfect condition seemed 'too good' to donate to Goodwill or the church thrift shop, especially when some extra cash was possible. Nobody wants to take it back home again - a lower price is still the better option for everyone - lucky you!

Never be afraid to ask for a better price.

Negotiating a lower price is expected in antique malls, secondhand shops, swap meets, flea markets, estate sales and garage sales. Here the best buys are always made by the shopper who knows how to bargain – and not shy about making offers. This is the land of individual stall vendors who have priced their items with margin for negotiation. They understand the game and are willing to play.

Bargaining doesn't have to be a confrontation. It can be a fun and elegant give-and-take, more like two dancers in a minuet rather than gladiators battling to the death. Many hardcore bargainers love the thrill of totally beating down the price - and their opponent. They are the gladiator types. They get great prices and strictly follow the rule of never paying too much. Dancer types prefer to follow Steven Covey's lead and walk away with a win-win.

It's easy to bargain when you find your own style.

How hard you bargain is up to you. With a little practice you discover it's easy to bargain when you find your own style. There are many factors: your personality, your empathy, how desperately you want whatever beautiful and priceless thing has caught your eye – and ultimately how much you can afford to pay. But bargain you must, if you want to pay the least - so you can buy more.

Don't know where to start? Just ask, "What is your best price?" It's as easy as that. No one is going to be insulted. If a vendor has a 'firm price' in mind, she might not be interested in coming down - yet. They usually hold 'new' merchandise awhile before they negotiate. But in the end, they are in business to sell and will give a 10-50% discount - just because you ask.

If you are shopping where different stall owners work the register or the floor for other vendors, don't hesitate to ask them to call the owner for her 'best price.' I brought home an arresting, life size, Greco-Romano bust with pedestal for $400 when the price tag read $875. I made the right offer when the seller was ripe. The price might have been higher (*or lower!*) on another day.

Antinous
- $400
including
pedestal

antique mall

DID YOU KNOW?

The first step in negotiating is easy.
Just ask "What's your best price?"
and see what they say.

You still have choices if the vendor holds to her firm price. You could just pay; the piece is unique or cheaper than anything at Dillard's. Or you could keep coming back until the vendor is hungry and ready to deal - but risk someone else buys it. I forfeited a drop dead gorgeous silver Saga Fox jacket to a Brit who flew home to London with my prize because I was waiting to pay $500 instead of $600 for a once-in-a-lifetime beauty. It was a risk and I lost. Always balance price against the strength of your desire.

Always balance price against the strength of your desire.

The optimal form of friendly bargaining emerges when you come to a price that you think is fair and good value and you sense the seller is also comfortable. It's very easy to tell. You part on friendly terms. Socially responsible win-win bargaining always ends with smiles on both faces. The vendor wants you to come back and gives you favorable prices when you do.

Win-win bargaining always ends with smiles on both faces.

A bargaining session might go something like this. You ask what the best price is. It's reasonable, so you counter below, but not too far. You don't come back at half. For example, you find a new Harley Davidson leather jacket at the swap meet that sells in the stores for $350. The seller says she was hoping to get $50, but she will let it go for $35. (*You know she needs money*).

New Harley Davidson leather jacket - $30

swap meet

It's a size 10, small for most women, so you have a strong advantage. You offer $30. You pushed back a little – but not too much. You don't offer $25. It's a steal and both of you know it. She grimaces a bit, pauses a moment and accepts your offer. She could hold fast at $35 and you would pay. But she's okay with $30, you got a little extra deal, and both of you are smiling when you hand over the money. You don't know what she paid for the jacket or where the jacket came from and you don't ask. It's just a happier world now.

When you see something you've absolutely got to have, you lose your advantage in bargaining. A hard core negotiator is always willing to walk away. If you can't walk, then your bargaining strength is gone. But if a wild and wonderful thing truly speaks to your soul, ask for the best price and be prepared to pay it. Although Zen shopping is about getting great prices, it's really about *getting what you want.* Don't get so caught up in winning that you lose.

Don't get so caught up in winning that you lose.

Some bargain hunters go for the jugular and their juices pump at the scent of a vendor's blood. It's a battle to the last penny. For the *winner-take-all* type, the greater the seller's pain, the sweeter the deal. It is more about paying as little as possible than desiring anything specific.

These shoppers often have lots of money and don't need to suck the life force from their opponent. This is serious business for gladiators, one in which their egos are intricately entwined. They always get the best prices, but they also walk away a lot – even from what they truly desire. Don't let that be you.

Your goal is to build long-lasting buy-sell relationships with vendors, the kind of win-win relationships that net you even better bargains in a sweet shopping future.

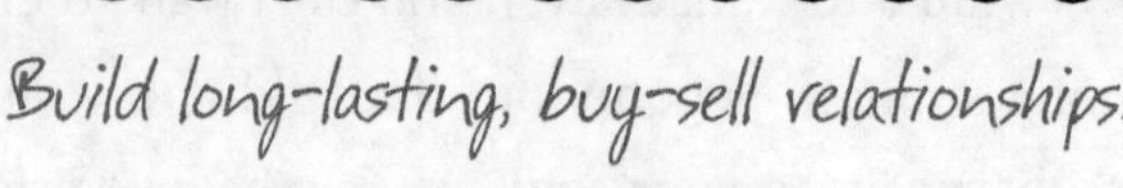

Chinese mirror
- $100
antique mall
So black with mold and dirt when purchased,
that flowers were but faint shadows.
Cleaned with index finger, cotton cloth and olive oil.

Step 4
go with the flow

Zen shopping can take you places you have never been and show you things you have never seen. The fun you have, the deals you strike, the relationships you forge, and the personal renewal you experience depend on your attitude and how flexible you are. The more adaptable you are, the more successful you are. It's a spontaneous odyssey, not a planned itinerary.

It's a spontaneous odyssey, not a planned itinerary.

The Zen way of shopping is not just whimsical and impulsive - although that's the best part. You can systematically revamp your wardrobe or upscale your home by being smart about where you shop and being patient about finding it. You can also clothe your family, replace a broken appliance and get your son a computer table on any budget.

You have the most fun when you go to the flea market just to see what you can discover. The best finds are always those you aren't looking for. Be open to what the Universe presents. "*Some days are just shoe days*" is the attitude for success. Give random a chance. Reinvent yourself with each new possibility.

"Give random a chance."

Georgia O'Keefe-style
Texas Long Horn skull and horns
- $79
antique mall

Step 5
you can do this!

You can develop any quality needed for success. Some you may already have, others you have to work on. There's not a quality listed here that wouldn't improve your life on every level, especially in a time when the best laid plans fall apart every day.

adventurous spirit. **You love the thrill of discovery.** You set out on every shopping trip into unknown territory without a map. You don't know what you'll find, but you are open to new ideas. You're willing to walk into unfamiliar spaces and situations, out of your comfort zone. The best finds are always found in the most unexpected places.

The best finds are always found in the most unexpected places.

patience. **You know things take time.** It's easy to walk into a department store and follow the subliminal messages directing you to buy. It's easy to pay the price on the tag. It might seem hard to dig through piles of junk to hit a jackpot. But with a little experience, you just know that the right dress, gloves, hat, dining room table, or painting is there waiting for you, somewhere. You keep looking. You're patient – and persistent - and discover other great treasures along the way. Have faith that you'll find exactly what the Universe knows you need.

You'll find exactly what the Universe knows you need.

open mind. **You are willing to take a chance.** You're not fixated on finding one particular item. You relax and let your mind receive the energy and perceive the possibilities as you connect with an object. You shop in places you never dreamed of before. Imagine a grand golden candelabrum at Goodwill for $3 that would be at home on any church altar and wonderful ablaze on Christmas Eve. Who knows why someone gave it away? But thank you, Universe, that they did!

self-confidence. **You are in charge.** Apparently it takes a lot of self-confidence to wear pre-owned clothes and old jewelry. This is an odd mindset, as a superior quality cut and fabric have intrinsic value just as any fine painting or tapestry. They are not diminished by history. Don't feel less of a person because your Ralph Lauren blazer cost you $11. You are not less, you are more – certainly more clever than the shopper who paid $250 for the same jacket.

Lamp
- $15
Marshalls
sale room

Antinous
- $400
antique mall

Lotus blossom
- $25/pair
estate sale

Flexibility. **You are an opportunist.** Searching for something specific, although achievable, can be frustrating. It's not the way the system works best. Look for elbow length white kid gloves and you might find 10 pairs – or none. Keep focused, keep looking and one afternoon you will find exactly the right ones that fit your hand like, well, a glove. Meanwhile, you happen upon a sexy black, hand-beaded evening sheath that clings seductively to your hips for $25 and you can't say "no" – and shouldn't. You mix it up with a jacket, a scarf, a vest; you have your basic black dress that gets you through the season(*s*) looking (*and feeling*) like a million bucks. Who would know you paid $25 unless you tell them?

appreciation. **You know quality.** You easily distinguish between the junk produced today – even with a respectable price tag - and the exquisite craftsmanship and excellence of materials you find in vintage. 'Not made in China,' unless it is supposed to be Chinese, like a carved screen, is such a blessing. There was *so* much more personality, originality and quality when mass merchandising didn't rule the day.

respect for history. **You connect with every object you explore.** It was created by a craftsman. It was owned by at least one, if not multiple persons, all with colorful and rich life stories. It may have traveled thousands of miles, across foreign lands and vast oceans to arrive in this tiny stall, awaiting your discovery.

traveled thousands of miles,
awaiting your discovery.

respect for people. **You savor interacting with people.** You befriend the vendors in antique, vintage and secondhand markets. This is their life; collecting is their passion. They have wonderful stories to share about every morsel in their stall – with a 100 times as many at home in their garage. For most it is a lifestyle that barely supports their obsession.

Happy and beautiful Claire doing what she loves.
antique mall

People everywhere are going through painful transitions. They are letting go of what they cherish, just as you have painfully let go of your old spending habits. It is often worse for them than for you. You, at least, are on the purchasing end. Showing humanity is a crucial part of the process.

Vintage wrought iron pheasants
- $25
antique mall

Step 6

six easy rules

Price is everything, especially when you have discerning tastes and not much money. Getting a killer deal on your heart's desire is what Zen shopping is all about. You can find beauty and quality for big bucks in lots of places. That's not hard. You did that for years.

#1 - always ask for a discount. Getting the right price is the single most important skill you need. Remember that the less you pay for one thing, the more you have to spend on something else. Always always try to get a lower price when you buy. Don't be timid to ask in any store. All they can say is "no."

Always always try to get a lower price when you buy.

Antonia strolls into Yves Saint Laurent in Copenhagen on a chilly May afternoon to ask for a discount on the summer sheath in the window. She blithely points out to the salesgirl that it's pouring rain and no Dane would buy a summer dress with temperatures in the damp 50's. It works. A quick phone call to the manager, who has often negotiated with Antonia - and the price is reduced 20%. It's one size 40 dress out of many; the sale is a win-win.

When I ask where she finds her bravura, she chuckles, *"What do I care what a shop girl thinks of me?"* This is exactly the kind of self-confidence you need.

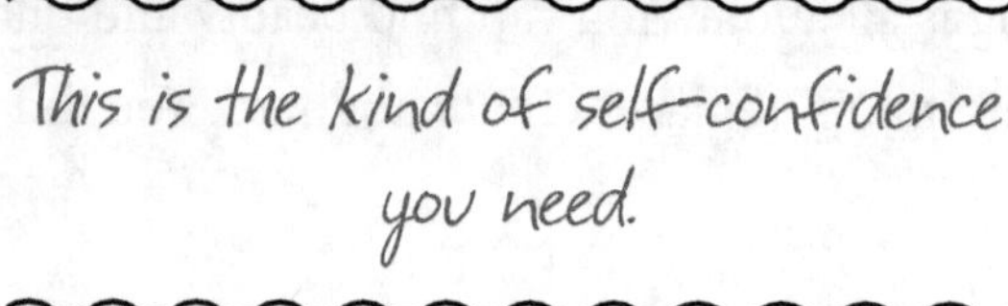

Thanks to lessons from Diva Antonia, I stole a yummy mint green and lavender leather sofa at 75% off in Santa Maria CA. My mantra? *"No one in the Central Coast is going to buy a sofa like this. It belongs in Palm Springs, Las Vegas or Miami Beach."* The manager agreed and subsequently gave me great deals on all the colored leather that stumbled into his otherwise oak furniture-filled warehouse. It was the wrong merchandise for his clientele, and I reaped the reward by pointing that out and being ready to buy when something exceptional showed up.

Try discounts off cardigans with slightly stretched buttonholes at Neiman Marcus and footstools with tiny scratches at Kohl's. You must talk to the manager to get approval, but it is well worth it. You were probably going to buy it anyway, so why not try to shave a little off the price?

Be respectful, but don't be intimidated by a salesclerk. You're just shopping smart, not dumb.

Learn to push back on prices without bullying. Striking a deal leaving both of you satisfied should be your goal. It's not hard to do. You don't insult; you don't condescend; you stop before the vendor gets mad—or looks like she wants to cry.

Learn to push back without bullying.

Unlike shopping in more exotic markets around the world, dramatizing faults is not a particularly successful bargaining tactic here in the U.S. It's okay to point out flaws in a retail store, but don't go too overboard at the antique mall. No one is fooled. If you didn't want the piece, you wouldn't have entered into the bargaining process. The vendor knows that. Americans don't play the negotiating games that are the norm in Hong Kong or Marrakech.

#2 - adapt to the environment. Connect with the array of cultures of the different shopping venues and adapt your negotiating and bargaining strategies. Always be polite and respectful. People are more responsive when they are feel comfortable and confident.

An employee does not have the same vested interest in a sale as an owner, unless they work on commission. If you are dealing with a fixed wage employee, ask to talk to the owner or ask them to call for you.

Commission-driven salespeople are highly motivated to strike a deal and will often go further than an owner, who might have an interfering emotional attachment. Owners can be the last to get realistic about the value of their property. You see that often in real estate. Good agents force buyer and seller to a common price, usually less than the seller wants and more than the buyer wants to pay.

People are more responsive when they feel comfortable and confident.

Garage, yard and estate sales are almost always owner-operated, although it is not uncommon for whole neighborhoods to band together for mega yard sales. You will generally get a better price from someone who is not the owner, but just wants to move the merchandise. Here is the place to gather a lot of stuff and make a package offer. This strategy is generally irresistible to the seller, even the owner. He has already come to terms with letting go of his possessions. He wants cash and he doesn't want to put anything back in the garage at the end of the day.

• • • • • • • • • • • • • • • • • •

DID YOU KNOW?

You get the best prices when you gather a lot of stuff and make a package offer.

• • • • • • • • • • • • • • • • • •

Luxury shopping calls for a different demeanor. It doesn't hurt to put on a few airs when asking for discounts at high-end stores. A commanding presence is always a plus in a place that deals in snobbism. You must act like you can easily afford to pay the full ticket, but that you are not the type of person to be taken advantage of. They assume that you will come back and buy plenty of merchandise at full price.

• • • • • • • • • • • • • • • • • •

DID YOU KNOW?

Luxury stores call for a slightly snobbish demeanor if you want to get a deal.

• • • • • • • • • • • • • • • • • •

Take it easy on people whom you can see are desperate or going through hard times. You'll see lots of them at your local swap meet. Be a good person and don't humiliate them more. You are sure to get an incredible price without much work at all. Be happy *you are you* - and not sitting in a tent on Saturday morning selling your cookware or a lifetime collection of Hummel porcelain figures.

Be happy you are you – and not selling your lifetime collections.

#3 – recognize quality. Train your eye to look for quality, whether in fabrics or craftsmanship. You find a silk velvet jacket for $30 or a full-length raccoon coat for $500. Slip your arms into those lush furry sleeves and imagine yourself at the Yale-Princeton game. Check out the lining, the inside of the pockets, the buttons. Look for worn places. Are they noticeable? Can they be fixed? If there is wear, you may have an opportunity to drive the price down. Most shoppers just want to put it on and go; they aren't interested in restoring, or even dry-cleaning.

You never regret buying anything in a color that speaks to your soul.

#4 – get in touch with color vibrations. Keep an eye out for colors that make you feel good or call out to you that day. Follow your instincts. You know what you like – and your instincts will tell you what you need. If you feel suddenly attracted to aquamarine, take a second look. If you see your favorite color - or a color that your spirit needs now in your life, take it home. You never regret buying anything in a color that speaks to your soul.

Esperanza
in a color that speaks to her soul.
Feathered 40's vintage hat (refreshed with new netting)
- $10 - antique mall

#5 - dress the part. The right outfit is an essential part of adapting to the culture. Dress up if bargain shopping at Saks, but dress way down when going to the swap meet. Leave your good jewelry and clothes at home when bargaining, especially if you know that the seller is probably coming from a weaker economic position. (*Count your blessings!*) It's hard to ask for $5 off when you have thousands on your fingers. Remember that you want to build rapport, not resentment.

You want to build rapport, not resentment.

#6 - budget yourself. Just because it is cheap and a 'great deal' doesn't mean that you won't be tempted to overspend. In fact, you see so many good deals that you must use more discipline than ever. Set a strict limit for yourself each shopping day. Force yourself to use your credit card only for that pre-determined amount and STOP. Best is to go cash-basis only. Take the cash you are willing to spend and spend no more when it is gone. This will hone your decision-making skills and temper your impulse buying.

No matter how broke you feel, you can always go shopping if you keep to the strict cash rule. You can find plenty to buy at a garage sale or antique mall for $15. You can come home from the Swap with a bag full of goodies.

No matter how broke you feel,
you can always go shopping.

You tend to buy as you go at the swap meet or flea market. It's hard to go back; maybe you can't find the spot again, or the item is quickly sold. A strict cash limit helps curb your impulse buying - too much, too soon, too fast.

You can hold things at the register if shopping in an antique mall. Check out is when you carefully evaluate your final

Tray
- $2
antique mall
Touched up with gold paint from Michael's.

purchases by measuring your needs and wants against your budget. You decide to let some things go (*for now*); you have the advantage of looking at the big picture rather than the mere snapshots that come with buying as you go.

Don't forget the layaway plan which allows you to pay cash over time for bigger ticket items. You delay the thrill, get more pleasure and still curb your shopping by using cash.

• • • • • • • • • • • • • • • • • •

DID YOU KNOW?

The best way to curb impulse spending is to pay only with cash.

• • • • • • • • • • • • • • • • • •

Esperanza dressed for success.

Oscar de la Renta leopard hat
- $60
antique store

Mink coat, full-length - new
- $2500
furrier - 'special' sale

Step 7
dress for success

Dressing for success in the bargain-hunting business is an integral part of adapting to the environment. As a general rule, you need to dress in a way that leaves you comfortable, agile and unencumbered.

Dress up only for the luxury store to get the respect you need for a strong bargaining position. Dress down for everything else. You aren't trying to impress. You are trying to get the best price. Remember the rule, *"The bigger the bargain, the more you hunt."* The hunting grounds can be dusty and crammed. Dressing lightweight, compact and in dark-colors is the rule for antique stores, vintage shops, yard sales, flea markets and the Swap.

You aren't trying to impress. You are trying to get the best price.

You want a stream-lined profile that moves easily through tight aisles flanked with precious glassware. Pick up a belly bag at a swap meet and leave your purse at home. Leave your coat/jacket in the car. They will just get in the way as you stoop down, dig through, and try on.

DID YOU KNOW?

You want to dress very stream-lined and keep your hands free. No purses, coats, bulky sweaters or clunky shoes.

Wear shoes that let you stand for hours and don't stumble around with big toes or clunky heels. You are sure to find purple velvet evening slippers or alligator cowboy boots - and your shoes need to slip off and on easily. Try old-fashioned Keds that cling to your feet like a dancer's Capezio's.

On your knees inspecting the bottom shelves of the glass case of vintage jewelry, evening purses and kid gloves, you want pants that let you stretch and move freely. The closer your clothes fit, the better. It makes it easier to try on that apricot silk blouse or squeeze down tight walkways to get a closer look at a faux (*maybe not!*) Ming vase.

You grab a hand-embroidered Spanish shawl and toss it around your shoulders right on the spot. Dressing rooms are usually in short supply in these locales, if they exist at all. At best it's far away or doubles as the ladies bathroom. You won't want to go back and forth with one item at a time, shedding layers of your own clothing for every impulsive look-see-try.

Shopping maven Esperanza from Las Vegas has perfected the art of dressing for serious shopping. In winter it's a tight-fitting black sweatshirt and black stretch pants. In summer it's black bike shorts and black tank top. With loosely laced Keds, a belly bag for cash and cell phone, short black gloves to protect manicured nails, and hair in a ponytail, everything about her screams, *"I'm a professional shopper"* - or cat burglar. Same work uniform required.

Essential swap meet gear is a sturdy canvas bag with handles generous enough to fit across the shoulders. Inside she tucks a handful of plastic bags to sort items and make everything compact. She hooks the straps across her shoulders and carries the cloth sack like a backpack when the loot begins to accumulate. This leaves her hands free. No constantly putting multiple bags down and picking them up again. The cloth sack is easy to slip off and on; it's less bulky and holds more than a backpack. And a folded cloth bag fits in the belly bag or tucks into a waist strap or belt until needed.

- Always wear comfortable shoes. You can't do your best hunting and bargaining when your feet hurt.
- Put on a hat and use sun block if you're outdoors at a swap meet or yard sale.
- Leave your good jewelry at home.
- Don't wear anything that would hurt you to see stained or torn.

"I'm a professional shopper."

Esperanza
'professional shopper'
with black gloves, Keds,
belly bag
and
canvas bag backpack.

Step 8
cash is king

Cash is always king, now more than ever. There is something about the sight of a greenback that sweetens a deal. The vendor not only saves on credit card fees, but profits from an off-the-books sale that bypasses the tax man. This is not to say that all antique and secondhand dealers are into avoiding taxes. But it's naïve to think that a $50 cash sale is always going to be reported. 25% more profit in a cash exchange that avoids sales and income tax and credit card fees naturally creates a more flexible bargaining environment.

DID YOU KNOW?

People respond differently to cash than to the abstract notion of plastic. The sight of a greenback sweetens most deals.

Cash doesn't have the same power if you get a cash register receipt. The records negate any tax advantage. You still have some edge as a cash sale saves the vendor the fees that credit card companies charge merchants for each sale.

The percentages are small, but can sometimes make a difference. Ask if there is a discount for cash rather than credit card. Cash here means the real thing, not checks. Vendors don't have the resources to track you down if the check bounces - and checks leave a traceable paper trail.

Iridescent blue billfold – $1 cash

swap meet

Cash is absolutely necessary at swap meets, flea markets, garage sales, estate sales and usually craigslist. Changing even a $20 bill can be cumbersome in these times. Get in the habit of carrying 10's and 5's - and always have a wad of dollar bills on hand for small purchases, food and tips.

Cash-only also makes it hard to overspend your budget. When it's gone, it's gone – and that's the kind of discipline you need to curb your shopping drive.

Making a big comeback is the layaway plan. It's a form of cash purchase, but over time. You make an initial cash payment and continue with installments until the item is paid off. You don't incur any interest, but you don't take anything home until it's completely paid off - which actually heightens the shopping pleasure and extends the thrill. The faster you pay down, the quicker your reward, thus thwarting other shopping - another way to curb spending. Department stores, discount stores and even antique malls all work with layaway plans. Ask if it's available.

Cash-only makes it hard to overspend. When it's gone, it's gone.

Grecian urn great for brandy. - $5

Salvation Army

let's get practical
what, where & how

The following chapters go into detail about what you can find, especially secondhand, and the best places to find it.

step 9 categorizes different things you might be looking for and where to find the best deals.

step 10 lists a variety of shopping venues and gives a detailed description of each, including advantages and disadvantages.

step 11 gives you tips on how you can buy less than perfect goods and refurbish them to your standards.

Black lamp
- $5
Goodwill

Red shade
- $7
Big Lots

Step 9

get everything you want

Everything can be found secondhand. Even the latest in electronics is already for sale on eBay at discounted prices. Houses, cars, art, jewelry, sporting equipment, evening dresses, and furs – it's all there just waiting for you to make yours.

Once you get over hang-ups about being the first owner, buying in a certain store and a specific label, or about *feeling poor*, you are free to take advantage of someone's need to turn worldly goods into cash. Their need creates your opportunity to buy higher quality for less money.

Once you get over hang-ups...you are free to take advantage...to buy higher quality for less money.

vintage clothing

Vintage clothing is all the rage, thanks partly to celebrities who discovered its wow power and had the courage to wear it - and admit it. They might be paying far more than you intend - or need to. But why shouldn't *you* own a Balmain gown?

The truly stunning designer dresses, bags, and hats are easiest to find in metropolitan areas with populations that would have purchased them new. Fashion rock star labels are naturally going to be rarer the further you get from Europe, New York, Los Angeles and San Francisco. But never assume that because you live in Peoria there will be no treasures in your local secondhand shop. Guaranteed something high quality made with luxurious fabric for cheap is there for you to discover.

Unless it's haute couture, the difference between secondhand and vintage is often just perception. But some ladies who wouldn't be caught wearing anything

Esperanza's collection (partial) of secondhand and vintage furs.
prices ranging from $30 - $500
antique malls, swap meets, secondhand stores, vintage shops

'secondhand' are able to take the leap if it's called 'vintage.'

hats, bags and gloves

Certain vendors specialize in vintage hats, although you are likely to find a couple in any antique stall. The selection ranges from the most chic Parisian pillbox to elegant white Panama's with wide brims – and everything in between: sunhats, berets, cloches, bonnets, Stetsons, fedoras and more. The selection in men's hats is astounding; once a necessary accessory for any man, almost no one under 70 or not a musician wears one today.

• • • • • • • • • • • • • • • • • •

DID YOU KNOW?

Nothing makes a statement like a stunning hat. It says you are a woman who values herself.

• • • • • • • • • • • • • • • • • •

Nothing makes a statement like a stunning hat. It's classy, daring and shows the world that you ooze self-confidence. Guaranteed you'll command attention in any room.

Vintage and just plain used bags are everywhere and often in good shape. You'll find the best ones in antique and vintage shops, although it is possible to stumble on a Gucci at the flea market. Sellers don't always know the value of what they have; they may have come by it in a less than legitimate way – or it's a knock off.

Esperanza is ready for Ascot.
Black straw hat - $30 - antique mall
Rhinestone earrings - $40 - antique mall
Prada sunglasses - $10 - swap meet

Bags and purses can be the most difficult vintage pieces to pull off. Unless you are out to achieve a 50's look, not all bags, even the best quality, can make the leap to now-time. It's far easier to tailor a dress than update a purse. But like all things vintage, you find truly superior craftsmanship and detailing in silk satin linings, patent leather clutches, and real leopard muffs.

Evening bags are the most versatile of vintage purses. They are generally classic in style and carried at night, making small imperfections less noticeable. They are the mainstay of many booths and can be found at dynamite prices for intricate bead and needlework.

If you're after a new bag, check out discount stores like Marshalls, Ross or Loehmann's. You'll mainly find low- to mid-quality, but enough designer labels and supple Italian leather to make it well worth your time. They buy up batches of inventory from designer brand distributors and sell at less than half, even a third of retail price. The purses can be from last season, or they can be part of an order that was cancelled by another store. A violet, faux alligator Dooney and Bourke handbag was $300 at Marshalls - pricey, yes, but compare that to $800 in luxury stores.

Loehmann's

DID YOU KNOW?
Discount stores like Marshalls or Loehmann's are the best source for new bags and purses - with some reasonable finds in shoes.

shoes and boots

Buying shoes in vintage stores can really be challenging. Women either used to have smaller feet — or those with big(ger) feet destroyed their shoes. But just as there are many secondhand shops that sell new clothes, some vintage vendors sell new shoes. Sizes are usually from 6-8, but there are no rules except that the inventory is limited. They had an opportunity to score a small lot of shoes, never worn, usually the same manufacturer, one size per style, and they pass the savings onto you.

Who knows where the shoes came from and why such an odd collection was there that Sunday? Does your conscience ask how and why? This is a moral issue you face when shopping off the grid, especially in swap meets and flea markets. You must decide if you can live with the answer once the question is posed. It's basically between you and your Shopping God whether you need to know - and what you do with the information.

The need for answers is between you and your Shopping God.

You'll find a nice selection of men's cowboy boots in secondhand and vintage stores, especially in the West. Women can wear men's boots, although they tend to run wide. The best selection in tooled leather, snakeskin, and alligator are always found in men's styles – at unbelievable prices. White ostrich boots for $40? Where else can you do that?

Goodwill and other thrift stores carry racks of shoes, in all sizes. You can even find new shoes that have been donated for a variety of reasons. The quality is not great, but as always, there are jewels - like $3 once-worn Clark loafers.

Buffalo Exchange is a nation-wide retailer that specializes in secondhand clothing and shoes. Their prices are reasonable and they operate like a typical boutique with exchange policies, credit cards, sales help and well-organized merchandise.

For new shoes, look to discount marketers like Marshalls, TJ Maxx, Ross and Loehmann's. You'll find good brands at half price, but rarely do you find superb quality. Some department stores have their own discount outlets, such as

Nordstrom's Rack. Macy's and Dillard's have ongoing shoe sales. Get familiar with your local department stores and get on their mailing lists to learn about special sale days and discounts for their cardholders.

non-vintage, secondhand clothing

The surest place to find quality used clothing is at a posh consignment shop, whether you are in Little Rock or Manhattan. Consignment shops and charity thrift stores are the main recycling centers for the ladies who shop regularly at Saks and Neiman-Marcus.

When they grow tired of, or grow out of, their designer label dresses, suits and coats, they head to a consignment shop to get a return on their investment. They may donate their hand-me-downs to a charity thrift shop, but are more likely to pass the higher-end clothing through a consignment store where a more appreciating buyer will take it home. Call it a desire for some cash combined with a 'pearls before swine' mentality.

Goodwill, Salvation Army and charity thrift stores are excellent places to pick up jeans, jackets, t-shirts, even formal dresses. You don't often find top quality as those items are usually recycled through consignment shops. The exception is thrift stores for high society charities and affluent churches. The selection at the East End Hospice

Thrift in the Hamptons or the Children's Cabinet Thrift at Lake Tahoe is about as good as it gets.

Check to see if you have Buffalo Exchange in your area. This is a nation-wide retailer, although mainly West Coast, specializing in secondhand clothing and shoes. You can find most anything in apparel and accessories, all in fine condition. Many of the styles are youthful; it *is* the perfect hunting ground for teenagers or the 20-something crowd. There is still plenty for every taste and age and should be on your list of regular shopping spots.

new clothing

Zen shopping isn't limited to vintage or secondhand. You can find great deals on totally new clothing alongside the used. The best finds are the classic styles of excellent quality that someone bought and never wore, perhaps in a hopeful frame of mind to lose weight - or they themselves couldn't resist a killer deal even in the wrong size. When they finally empty their closet, a handful of Ralph Lauren blazers end up at an antique mall. Never worn, pockets still stitched, they range in price from $11-$25.

Do you have to dig? Yes. Do you have to keep going back? Yes. Do you usually find great buys at the same places? Yes, but not always. Some finds are simply once in a lifetime opportunities.

DID YOU KNOW?

You can find great deals on totally new clothing at secondhand and vintage stores and the swap meet and flea market.

The best vendors have a keen eye and have developed excellent sources over the years. They have good taste, understand quality, know what sells and how to price. Develop a relationship with them. They can keep an eye out and give you a call when they see something in your style. The more you buy, the more often you buy, the better the prices. Repeat customers are priceless commodities.

Ann Klein silk blouse - $5

Ralph Lauren blazer - $11

Louis Vuitton silk scarf - $25

vintage clothing stall antique mall

New t-shirts
- $2 each at the swap meet

• • • • • • • • • • • • • • • • • • •

DID YOU KNOW?

The more often you buy from one vendor, the better your prices.

• • • • • • • • • • • • • • • • • • •

You can find masses of new clothing at the swap meet or flea market - at rock bottom prices, all cash, no sales tax - or return policies. The vendor may be selling a thousand t-shirts for $2 each or a single suede coat for $50. Merchandise comes from everywhere and every circumstance – legitimate and otherwise. It's as close to a truly free market economy you'll find anywhere in America. It's the Wild West of shopping.

jewelry

Some of the best buys of all Zen shopping are found in the jewelry cases of antique and vintage shops. It approaches the divine to experience the color, the sparkle, the variety, and the originality found in the art of jewelry making. Most of the selection is costume jewelry, but you'll also discover locked cases with gold, silver and precious stones, including diamonds. Don't expect certification; if you're not an expert, you have to trust the vendor.

estate jewelry is the prized specialty of many antique dealers and jewelers. Called *estate* because the source was traditionally through death and inheritance, it has come to mean vintage jewelry of a higher quality, often made from precious metals and gemstones. If you buy from a licensed jeweler, you should receive an accurate appraisal and certification of stone quality and precious metal karat. These items are often on consignment, with the price firm until the owner consents to a discount. Ask the vendor for a better price just as you would anywhere else.

Keep in mind that cleaning enhances the hidden beauty of many vintage pieces. There are also electroplating companies that specialize in refurbishing jewelry metals and can restore a worn golden armband to original luster.

DID YOU KNOW?

Pawn shops are the best source of diamonds and watches. Shop here if you think in hundreds or thousands of dollars as a bargain.

pre-owned jewels are flooding the market with everyone looking for ways to raise cash and emptying their jewelry boxes to do so. Pawn shops are brimming with quality pre-owned jewelry, especially diamond rings and luxury watches, at less than wholesale prices. With a fresh new supply of desperate people, they have a large selection in stock. You find Rolexes and 2-karat solitaires at prices *very* reasonable for what you are getting. Shop here if you think in hundreds (*or small thousands*) of dollars as a bargain.

Pawn shops are quite good at appraising value; they are in the business of loaning money with the item as collateral. A larger shop often has a jeweler on staff to determine how much they are willing to loan vs. how much they believe they can recoup if the item goes for sale. Ask for an authenticated appraisal for gemstones or expensive watches. You'll need it for insurance. A reputable pawn shop (*they do exist!*) should have no problem with that.

funky costume jewelry makes up surprising collections at Goodwill, Salvation Army and other thrift stores - on sale for next to nothing. They only display pieces that function - no broken clasps. You won't find much of value as good jewelry is something you can easily turn into cash. But it's always worth a look. People get rid of the most amazing things, sometimes valuable. They don't want the work of a yard sale and feel good about supporting a favorite cause by recycling to the more needy – which might just be you!

furniture

Consignment shops not only carry secondhand furniture for sale by individuals, but also floor models from other furniture stores and furniture marts. The quality of furniture is better than you find at Goodwill and likely cheaper and more modern than at an antique mall. Price tags generally note the date the item first went on sale. Always check that date. The longer time the item has been on the floor, the greater the discount.

• • • • • • • • • • • • • • • • • •

DID YOU KNOW?

Consignment shops date the arrival of each piece. Discounts get deeper as time goes by.

• • • • • • • • • • • • • • • • • •

Not really looking for a sofa, I spied a red suede cloth, Bauhaus modern beauty with silver art nouveau legs marked $525. It had been on the floor for three months and the owner was pleased to let it go for $400 - a win-win deal. The Universe brought this sofa into my life, and I decided to act. It was the springboard that focused the

Red sofa - $400
consignment shop
Pillows - $15 ea - Marshalls
Zebra area carpet - $100 - close out sale

design direction of my new condo - a zebra carpet bought on closeout, a gray leather lounge chair from Marshalls and a red Chinese mirror from an antique mall.

note: Furniture consignment shops may offer delivery service for a fee, especially if they are connected to a regular retail vendor.

used contemporary furniture – especially desks and bookcases - is where craigslist really shines. The pieces advertised are typically inexpensive and in good shape. Craigslist attracts the buyer who expects to pay cash for an item that requires no fixing up and can be used immediately with no effort. It's a market concerned more with functionality than uniqueness, but there are no hard and fast rules about what you can find – *anywhere.*

antique immediately brings to mind *old* and *costly*. To qualify strictly as an antique, that *escritoire* must be 100+ years old and handmade. It doesn't have to be beautiful, but usually is. It should be of excellent quality and craftsmanship. It can be American, European or Asian. Like buying diamonds in a pawn shop, bargains in antiques are everywhere, but too rich for most budgets. Much furniture called antique is simply older and made of solid wood. If the price is right, and you like it, it doesn't matter if it truly qualifies as antique. What you want to avoid is paying antique prices for just old.

What you miss in selection, you make up for in serendipity.

A real antique or not, it doesn't matter if you like it. The key is not to pay antique prices for just old.

swap meets, flea markets, and garage and estate sales are the true mother lodes for bargain priced loot no matter what you are looking for - including furniture. Most of the 'stuff' is just that - a bizarre and eclectic array of odds and ends of varying quality, much in need of TLC and fantasy. But what you miss in consistent selection, you make up for in serendipity.

Swap meets and flea markets sell new and used furniture at the cheapest prices possible. Their overhead is as low as it gets. Merchandisers with regular retail outlets may operate side businesses on the weekends at the Swap and may be set up to take credit cards. Otherwise expect to pay cash and arrange for delivery yourself.

New strollers and baby seats at the swap meet.
As cheap as it gets.

estate sales are usually yard sales in better neighborhoods. They can, however, signify a wealthy grandmother passing to the next world and her heirs passing on her worldly goods to you. Here's your chance to find better quality furniture, maybe some artwork or crystal for a good price. This is where many antique dealers get their merchandise.

They hit the estate sales first thing in the morning; they take away the best pieces to resell with a finder's fee. You can cut out the middle man by being there yourself – early.

• • • • • • • • • • • • • • • • • • •

DID YOU KNOW?
'Estate sale' is code for a yard sale in a better neighborhood.

• • • • • • • • • • • • • • • • • • •

Goodwill, Salvation Army and other charity/church thrift stores are stocking more furniture, but quality goes very fast. Look for bookcases, TV stands, baby beds, kitchen table sets and patio furniture - maybe in need of some TLC - but usually nothing more than a change of knobs or quick paint re-touch.

Step 10
the best hunting grounds

You can find a bargain almost anywhere today. A Zen shopper doesn't discriminate. You don't set boundaries on where to hunt. You have moved beyond elitism; you're out to score the best deal wherever and whenever you find it.

Antiques at the Market

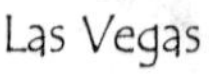
Las Vegas

You'll have the most fun with a shopping partner – someone who loves the sport as much as you do. Together you'll be more daring and explore more adventurous locales. She'll point out things you would have missed. Not to mention that a little competition fuels the hunting spirit, and instant bragging rights make it all the more satisfying.

Sana at Seaside Collectibles - Shell Beach CA

Where you look for bargains depends on what you need or want. Every shopping venue has its advantages, disadvantages - and opportunities. Each is discussed in detail in the pages that follow, arranged in alphabetical order. Use the index (back of book) to search for specifics.

new:

- Box stores - Target, Walmart, Kmart etc.
- Department & retail stores
- Discount stores - Marshalls, Ross, Loehmann's etc.
- Internet shopping sites
- Outlet malls
- Travel jewelry (knock off jewelry)

secondhand, vintage, antique:

Antique & collectibles shops

Antique malls

Auctions

Consignment shops

Estate sales

Garage sales, yard sales and moving sales

Pawn shops

Secondhand stores

Swap meets and flea markets

Thrift stores, Goodwill and Salvation Army

Vintage clothing stores and websites

both new and secondhand:

Antique malls

craigslist

Classified ads

eBay

Home parties – gold parties

Secondhand stores

Swap meets and flea markets

Thrift stores, Goodwill and Salvation Army

Vintage clothing stores

Find a shopping partner – someone who loves the sport as much as you do.

antique malls

Shop for: Vintage, used, and antique furniture, collectibles, art, clothing.
Always negotiate for best price.

Cashier counter at 'Antiques at the Market' - Las Vegas

Antique malls are a treasure trove for the bargain hunter of art, furniture, glassware, jewelry, clothing, and books - antique, vintage and simply secondhand. The prices tend to be far more reasonable than in an individual antique store and the selection, at times, wonderfully overwhelming.

Individual shop owners and collectors rent space under one roof, sharing the tasks of cash register and customer service. You'll find very few vendors actually on site, with many stalls (mini-shops) unmanned. They have excellent security though, and you will be on camera.

If something is in a locked case, usually jewelry or fine glassware, ask one of the staff to open it. Don't ever hesitate to ask. Vendors all love their work and enjoy sharing the tactile experience with you. Think of being in a museum where you can actually touch, with the curator standing by. Spontaneity is definitely dampened, but you should still treat browsing just as you would anywhere. Don't feel obligated in any way because it took a few minutes to get access to the Victorian garnet ring.

Always bargain at an antique mall. Occasionally something will be marked '*firm*.' Ignore that. The term 'firm' is often used to separate out a special piece from the rest of the inventory on which the vendor is offering a blanket discount of 20-50%. Everything in that booth is discounted automatically at the register except when marked firm. If you like it and want it, always make an offer. The staff will call the owner and see what she says. She could really mean *firm* - or she might like what she hears and be ready to sell for less.

• • • • • • • • • • • • • • • • • •

DID YOU KNOW?

A 'firm price' may mean the vendor is so attached she doesn't want to bargain, or it may separate an object from blanket discounts on the rest of the merchandise. In reality, there is no such thing as a firm price in the secondhand business. With time, everything is open to negotiation.

• • • • • • • • • • • • • • • • • •

Always check that a posted or agreed upon discount is given at the register when rung up. The cashier is another vendor fulfilling an obligation to the co-op and not profiting from overcharging you. Honest mistakes and oversights can and do happen – quite frequently.

A good antique mall is like a museum where you not only have pleasure in viewing, but also caressing. Everything has a history; there are infinite stories waiting for your imagination to unveil. You can spend hours poring over display cases of cameos, trying on Schiaparelli pillbox hats, and admiring jade Buddhas. Unique pieces, tiny and large, from faraway places fill every nook and cranny.

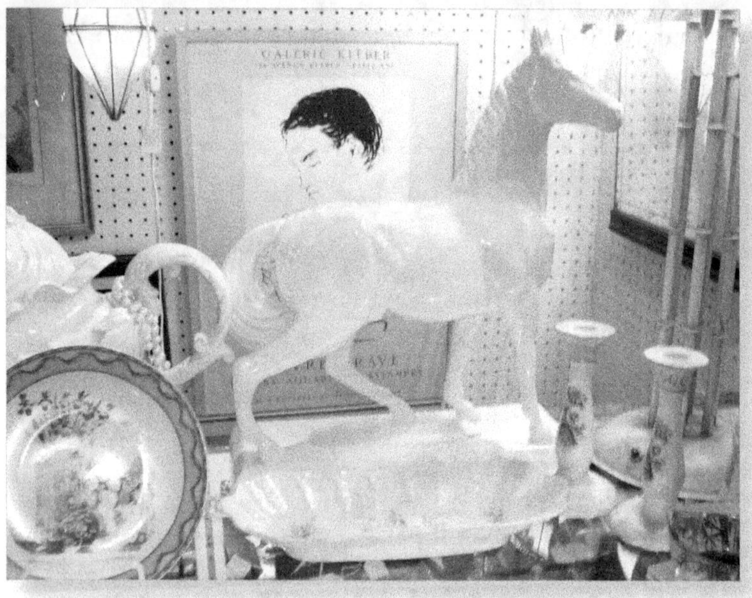

Make the vendor happy.
Tell her, "I love him! He's going to a good home."

The antique mall is where you want to make the personal connections that bring you good prices and preferential treatment. Show appreciation for a collection. It represents the vendor's life and they are passionate about every piece they display. The stories they can tell!

Items in antique malls tend not to move fast; you usually have a chance to go back again and bargain. It took me several visits before I managed to nab my bust of Antinous at half the asking price. I risked that someone else would be as smitten as me and snap it up before I got back. The gamble was part of the thrill of the hunt; it was doubly sweet when he finally came home with me.

A good antique mall or shop is like a museum - except you can touch.

Antique malls are also home to collectibles like dolls and Star Trek figurines, country crafts, newly-sewn velvet shawls and robes, and contemporary handmade silver jewelry. There are few restrictions as to what is sold as long as the rent is paid on the booth. Individual vendors decide if their kind of buyer will shop at that mall.

The best antique malls are dedicated to antiques and vintage collectibles, taking pride in unique, one of a kind inventory. These special malls cater to the discerning customer who knows and expects quality and originality.

The more 'country' and 'new,' the more the mall caters to tourists - and sometimes the more in trouble financially. But you can find treasures hidden in quiet corners even in malls overburdened with quilts and garden accessories. These can be your best finds; few appreciate their value and with no competition, they can be yours for a song.

Some antique malls feature more 'country' than vintage.

antique & 'collectibles' shops

Shop for: Quality furniture and art
- or old, used and vintage
- or eclectic bric-a-brac & tsatskes
- or "country" in rural antique stores.
Don't pay antique for just old.

Antique stores generally fall into three categories: authentic, 'collectibles', and tourist trap. The authentic antique shop is known for the priceless and the over-priced - an intimidating place to anyone who doesn't feel wealthy. The catch-all name 'collectibles' describes that cozy kind of shop with a lush and eclectic assortment of bric-a-brac and *tsatskes*. The tourist shop is geared to country and homemade crafts, often punctuated with painted wooden chests, cupboards and rocking chairs.

• • • • • • • • • • • • • • • • • • •

DID YOU KNOW?

'Antique shop' does not mean that everything is really old and very expensive. There are many small treasures, especially in finely crafted heirloom tsatskes.

• • • • • • • • • • • • • • • • • • •

Anyone can call themselves an antique dealer - the use of *antique shop* is unregulated. Never hesitate to check out a shop advertising 'antiques' just because you have a preconceived notion that the name on the door signals that everything in the shop will be super expensive and not subject to negotiation. Remember you can always stumble on a deal, no matter where you shop.

DID YOU KNOW?

Antique is not a regulated term and anyone can hang up a sign claiming 'Antique Shop.'

The term 'antique' is widely over-used with hopes of attracting a higher quality clientele willing to pay inflated prices. It should describe a quality piece that is handcrafted and over 100 years old. The term has been stretched to encompass almost anything old in secondhand furniture and crafts. The phrase '*going antiquing*' covers everything from antique mall browsing to exploring swap meets and elicits appealing sensations of discovery and richesse.

You can always stumble on a deal, no matter where you shop.

Antique stores in the center of big cities are generally the real deal. A bargain hunter on a tight budget won't find much there. But if you have good taste and extra cash, you can ferret out some really exquisite bargains right now. All levels of society are feeling pain, so just as in real estate, the cash buyer in antiques and art can scoop up high value for a fraction of its previous cost.

The market in European antiques is extremely depressed, with the younger, more affluent crowd preferring retro-50's to George III. The older wealthy, who would be more inclined to purchase classic antiques, are deciding they have enough already and their children aren't interested.

Chinese and Russian pieces are hot properties, as those newly rich nationals are on a quest to repatriate the wealth and beauty of their culture that found its way to the West during colonial times or after revolutions. You'll see these buyers at the big auction houses where the most valuable antiques and works of art are sold. You will also compete with them in the antique stores of New York, Rome, Paris, and London.

Antique stores in rural areas tend to be more 'country' than vintage or antique. They often stock new, handmade items with an emphasis on locally made. Geared towards selling to tourists, they carry crafts such as quilts, wooden and painted carvings, incense, candles and souvenirs. More than antique, these 'country stores' are peddling cultural authenticity.

DID YOU KNOW?

'Antique stores' in rural areas more often sell country-style, local, homemade crafts than anything vaguely antique.

'The Nest'
San Luis Obispo CA

Seaside Collectibles - Shell Beach CA

auctions

Bid for: aerospace memorabilia, dinosaur fossils, cars, houses, office equipment, boats, stamps, coins, art, books, jewels, junk. Almost anything of any value.
For budgets of $100 to $1,000,000+

There is nothing quite as exciting as an auction - or sometimes as sad. A family farm on the block is a great place to pick up a wheat thresher, but not a joyful occasion. Much more fun is the police auction where fancy cars, watches and boats seized in drug busts are sold off to the highest bidder. No pulling at heart strings here, just a licking of chops at deals that really grab your attention.

Of course, you need quite a bit of mad money for the high end auctions which offer rare bottles of 1964 Clos Vougeot *Gros Freres et Soeur* (red Burgundy) or an Apollo 14 dust brush used on the lunar surface. For the connoisseur with money in the bank, now is the time for a marvelous shopping spree in everything from Isfahan oriental carpets to an Eocene (30 million years+) fossilized palm leaf. Final bids are often half the catalogue price range.

You don't have to be a millionaire to score something rare and wonderful, but only need a couple extra thousand dollars to bring home museum quality artifacts.

If your budget is more moderate, check out bankrupt companies going out of business. These auctions are less glamorous, but rich sources for bargain-priced photocopy machines, desks and file cabinets. Antique stores closing their doors often auction off their collectibles by the cardboard box, like grab bags of eclectic goodies going for as little as $20.

Winning the bid at an auction is a thrill like no other. From the opening bid right through the subtle, yet breath stopping, back and forth between bidders to the sound of the final gavel and the burst of applause, a spirited auction can be as suspenseful as any tennis match at Wimbledon.

You'll find local auctions advertised in the newspaper and online. Just google "auction" to see offerings from foreclosed properties to fine art. You can even participate in live online auctions.

If you are after the best of the best, visit the websites of famous houses like Bonhams, Christie's, or Sotheby's. If nothing else, you can drool over their catalogues.

http://www.bonhams.com
http://www.christies.com
http://www.sothebys.com

box stores - Walmart, Kmart, Target

Shop for: Any item bought for sheer functionality.
This is not the place to go for anything not made in China.
Think blenders and socks.

These mass consumer outlets no doubt have good prices, although quality tends to be just good enough for utility. You certainly don't need any guidance about shopping at Walmart – just about everyone in America on a strict budget already does. But it is not the place to go for originality and style.

Of this genre of store, Target alone has made a commitment to appeal to a more fashion conscious type of shopper who lovingly refers to it as *Tar-jay* (French-fried pronunciation) – a tongue in cheek way of describing mass market, cheap shopping gone trendy.

Shopping at Target or the Walmarts of the world can work for very practical items. If you want a new blender, then it's the place to go - or Costco or Sam's Club. But don't forget to check out your local thrift store or yard sale for *really* cheap pricing on a used but fully operational model.

Target and Costco run specials that are advertised on their websites. If you sign up for their mailing list, you will receive frequent updates and the newest offers.

By all means, go for the deals in box stores when functionality and price are all that matter. But generally steer clear of the mass produced clothing and household items sold there. My advice is to head for *anywhere else*. The bargains on much higher quality are out there at prices that compete.

http://www.target.com
http://www.costco.com

classified ads

Shop for: Anything old or new in your geographic area.
Quickly being replaced by internet except in smaller local markets.

The printed newspaper is in its last death throes. Readership is down and ad sales have plummeted as the modern world moves to the computer for both news and marketing. That translates to more opportunity for the bargain shopper. Those who are still selling through the classifieds are from another mindset, a bygone era. They are not reaching full market potential, which could signal an opportunity for you to find better prices.

This is where you look when you live in a smaller community that wouldn't be covered by craigslist. This is where you look when you want a particular item and you need it now. This is also where you look when you want to price compare, analyzing offerings in the local paper with any on craigslist.

There are some advantages to local ads. First, they are updated weekly. A seller will not continue an ad if the item has been sold. You can also 'compare shop' more easily as classified ads group similar items together, rather than in loose categories and by date posted as on craigslist.

A local paper whose circulation is a small geographic area almost guarantees the seller is a short distance away.

consignment shops

Shop for: High quality, secondhand designer clothing and accessories.
Wait for price reduction unless you are in love.

Here's a chance to really hit pay dirt when it comes to finding high quality, designer label clothing discarded by the rich (and sometimes famous.) You might find anything in a consignment shop and very often the best of the best.

Consignment shops recycle the merchandise that some people consider too valuable to donate to their church thrift shop. The asking price can be on the high side for secondhand, but if the item doesn't move, the shop will negotiate. Clothing, furniture, jewelry, shoes and accessories are marketed as in any secondhand shop, except the owner gets a percentage of the sale only when the pink mink is sold.

There is usually an agreed upon time frame limiting how long the jacket will be held in stock - and before a price reduction. It could be one to three months or more, depending on the store policy and the item. Furs in July have far less value than in October. If the mink vest still doesn't sell, even at a discount, the owner gets it back – and chances are very strong she doesn't want that.

DID YOU KNOW?

Consignment shops are the best place to buy secondhand top designer labels at deep discounts.

Consignment shops are hands down the greatest opportunity to score top designer labels at deeply discounted prices, but you may have to be patient to wait for the discount and have the nerves to risk that someone else is willing to pay the full ticket price. You can always offer something less than the asking price and see what happens.

The longer the item has been in the store, the more interested all parties are in seeing it go. The boutique wants to be brimming with new and exciting items every time a shopper visits; the owner wants cash and tires of waiting.

But if you are totally in love, then buy when you see it. The asking price is bound to be far less than when first purchased at Saks.

craigslist

Shop for: Used and new home office furniture, bookcases, golf clubs, computers, cars, roommates, jobs.
Think practical stuff found in your geographic area.

A genius idea created by Craig Newmark for the San Francisco market as a free online marketplace in lieu of classified ads, craigslist is an entirely internet-driven exchange that has mushroomed into a national database with offerings from home sales to job opportunities. Although the site is national, it functions on a local level with postings sorted first by city (geography), then by category, and finally by date posted.

You can literally find anything on craigslist, from a roommate to a bookcase - even a wonderful home for two cats when moving from a beach house in California to a condo in Vegas. The beach house was rented to a woman in New Jersey on the second day of posting on craigslist. A student rental in California went in 24 hours to architecture students in Florence, Italy just finishing their junior year abroad.

The items you find for sale on craigslist are typically in ready-to-use condition and should be driving distance from where you live. You will be expected to pay cash and manage pick-up and delivery of anything you buy. There are many similarities between buying on craigslist and buying from a classified ad in your local newspaper, including paying cash and assuming risks – no money back guarantees and usually no returns.

Craigslist allows you to search by city, view a photo and read non-cryptic descriptions with information and conditions the seller wants to pass on.

This is the favorite site of the under-40 crowd in large metropolitan areas. It fulfills most of their needs. Find a job, find a place to live, and then furnish it.

Offers on craigslist are posted by individual sellers. There is no fee to list or sell the offer and no charge for you to look or buy. Log in first to the geographic area that interests you, then the category you are looking for. Contact the vendor by clicking on the link in the post and sending an email message to craigslist, which is then forwarded to the seller. The seller may choose to put his direct contact info in the post, but most don't.

Postings in each category, usually with a photo, are displayed in chronological order, the most recent at top.

You may need to scroll through many days to find what you are looking for - and the best prices. Postings are removed by craigslist after a certain period of time or by the seller himself. Sellers are notoriously slow about taking a post down after a sale, so don't assume it's available just because it's still up. Don't be surprised either if you never hear back. Most ignore emails once they have made their deal.

With the demise of the printed press, craigslist and similar sites are the places the savvy go first to find secondhand deals on specific items, especially anything contemporary and practical.

Go to: **http://www.craigslist.com** and click on the geographic area and the category you seek.

http://www.craigslist.com

department & retail stores

Shop for: Any new clothing item, shoes, fashion accessories, household goods, giftware.
Only buy on sale.

This is obvious and doesn't need much explanation. With stores closing or discounting deep to move merchandise, there are some incredible deals to be had.

Visit your local mall and check out stores that are shutting their doors. They are generally not shy about advertising, but don't always spend what it takes on media to get the word out. Ads in the local newspaper are one source, but your best bet is to talk to other shoppers when you are at a sale. The word spreads fast among bargain hunters; most are more than willing to share information. Don't be shy. Strike up conversations. You have a common interest – you are all hunters thirsting for a killer deal.

Check for special deals at the national department stores. They can sometimes be quite regional in their offerings. Macy's runs sales campaigns that rival any bargains at a discount store with the added pluses of organized merchandise and accommodating sales help. All departments are discounting at all times, although not with all merchandise. Clerks direct you to sale items and advise you that prices will be lower on Tuesday - or that the 400-thread count Egyptian cotton sheets will be on sale next week. They point out a similar set on sale now, so unless you have a penchant for one brand – enough that you are willing to pay full price rather than half for equal quality– there are bargains galore every day.

• • • • • • • • • • • • • • • • • •

DID YOU KNOW?

A balance on a store credit card means you can pay interest rates of 24% or higher. Any discounts evaporate, which is how the store makes money on sales – and you.

• • • • • • • • • • • • • • • • • •

Look for deep discounts on items that are not good sellers in that geographic region - like knee-high faux python boots in rural Oregon or mink jackets in Florida.

Get a 'most favored card' from a department store to reap the benefits of discount coupons and money back offers. **Never** carry a balance or all your discounts vanish - *poof!* Best is to use layaway - cash only, no interest and you still get what you want - and have more time to savor the thrill.

discount stores

Shop for: New clothing, shoes, bags, cosmetics, household goods, some furniture, wall decorations, bric-a-brac Good source for coffee, tea, chocolate, and gourmet condiments & jams.

Marshalls, TJ Maxx, Ross, Nordstrom's Rack, Burlington Coat Factory, Tuesday Mornings and others of this genre are a rich source of bargain pricing on new merchandise. A few lucky souls have Loehmann's, the primo of all discount stores, in their city.

Store location plays a big role in determining selection. Marshalls in Arroyo Grande CA will carry slightly different merchandise than Olathe KS, although the general quality remains constant. There is a great deal of very cheaply made clothing at bargain prices. But you can also find name designers - if you look hard. Some call it 'rack-shopping' with an air of disdain – I call it smart shopping.

End of season, returns, and unsold goods are usually their supply source. The merchandise is sent to them through their central distributor and often is random enough that the employees themselves are as dazzled by new arrivals as you might be. Nordstrom's has its own discount outlet, aptly named Nordstrom's Rack, with a fabulous shoe and sunglass collection. It's just pure *nirvana* for the smart 'rack shopper.'

Loehmann's is the primo of all discount label shopping.

downtown San Francisco

Most people equate clothing and shoes with Marshalls, TJ Maxx and Ross, but bargain prices for reasonable quality are also found in their home and cosmetic departments. Look for name brand lotions and perfumes, as well as a fair selection of chairs, carpets, mirrors and wall hangings.

Include Tuesday Mornings in the above group and *always* look for towels, kitchenware, photo frames, and glassware before shopping elsewhere. There is no point paying full price for *any* of these items. Selection is limited. You must choose among what they have - and what they have this week, they may never have again. If you need more of a specific item, ask the clerk to call other stores in your area. This is a case for buying it when you see it – it may be your only chance.

Buy it when you see it; it may be your only chance.

Shop for spices, jams, coffee, tea, olive oil and vinegar along with gourmet teas, chocolates and cookies. The selection is most impressive at holiday time when the shelves overflow with European imports, especially Italian and English. This is the place to find the perfect hostess gift for holiday parties. Long shelf life items like pancake and soup mixes, Bar-B-Q sauces, pickles, jams, syrups, condiments, candies and cookies are stocked year round.

DID YOU KNOW?

Marshalls and Ross have great prices on English tea, Greek olive oil, Belgian chocolate, and Italian biscuits.

If you still need more stuff to hang on your walls or set on your mantelpiece, you won't want to miss the aisles abundant with icons of Egyptian Nefertiti, Chinese Buddha and other statues, vases, lamps, floral arrangements, bookends – and even books, especially travel and cooking.

An ebony kneeling Pharaoh fools everyone as a valuable artifact from my trips to the Nile – until they lift it and see the Ross tag on the bottom and 'made in China.' I could remove the tag and perpetuate the ruse, but it's more fun to see the surprise (and awe) on their faces.

Faux Pharaoh
– $15
Ross

Most stores have dedicated areas or special sale rooms set aside for items that are discounted even further. *Head there first* to get the best deals. Impulse buying is everyone's temptation, so allow yourself a little extra mad money when you're out to replenish your stash of Yorkshire tea or Kauai coffee. Who can resist a classical Kool-Aid glass pitcher with blue glass handle for $6?

"Kool Aid" pitcher - $6 Marshalls sale room

Tuesday Mornings specializes in household goods, often the identical items found at Marshalls or Ross, and with a surprising variation in price - sometimes higher and sometimes lower. Price comparing is smart shopping, but although it may pay to check out several stores before purchasing a set of cookware, rarely does it make sense to burn a lot of gasoline to save a dollar or two on one item.

eBay

Shop for: New and secondhand everything, but especially collectibles.
Find anything anywhere.
Learn special skills for online auction bidding.

eBay lies at the heart of the internet shopping revolution. Set up as an online auction with national and even global potential for exposure, it has grown to be the definitive site to buy and sell single unusual items. Look for eBay-linked shopping sites with diverse inventories as well.

This is not a place to shop if you yearn to touch the things you buy. If shopping is a kinesthetic experience for you, tactile and sensual, then you will better enjoy the antique mall or swap meet. But if you are looking for specific gold coins to round out your collection, you can't beat eBay.

eBay developed ways to pay safely online - as safe as exists. The US Post Office and UPS facilitate shipping. It has also developed a vendor rating system that eliminates most fraudulent activity.

Sellers post photos of their products. There is usually a return policy if you are not satisfied when you open the box your mailman delivers. Most sellers are anxious to keep their favorable rating. eBay is a livelihood for many; they understand the importance of customer service. If eBay vendors slip in their ratings, they risk losing future sales on a global scale. This is not to say you can't run across a flake. There are no guarantees, but the eBay shopping experience scores very reliable on the shopping scale.

eBay started as an online auction and auctions are still a staple of its sales. Auctions against other online bidders involve placing your bids, watching the competition and making new bids if necessary - a timing strategy very specific to eBay. Auctions where no one else is bidding bring some great buying opportunities. There are also many items for straight sale, with no bidding at all.

eBay is a veritable Mecca for collectors looking for very specific items. The world is your marketplace. If you know what you are looking for – anything that you could ever imagine - you will certainly find it and at the most competitive price.

Go to: **http://www.ebay.com** and click on the category.

http://www.ebay.com

estate sales

Shop for: secondhand bikes, golf clubs, baby gear, kitchen appliances, lawn furniture, tools, pool tables, art, crystal, clothing, sometimes antiques.

Usually just a yard sale in a 'better' neighborhood.

Look for *estate sale* if you want better quality castoffs than you find at a typical garage sale. The term is pretty much code for 'better neighborhood yard sale,' used instead of *yard* or *garage* sale in hopes of attracting a more affluent clientele.

Originally, an estate sale occurred when someone died and left an estate – a term that in itself implies value. Authentic estate sales do exist if you live in the right areas of the country. But the items of considerable value are normally sold through organized auctions, if the heirs have any smarts at all.

Although an estate sale is simply a glorified garage sale in most cases, it doesn't diminish their promise. You'll find the same types of things as in a yard sale, but generally of higher quality and in better condition. Look for good costume jewelry, interesting books, nice artwork and even a piano, guitar, pool table or pinball machine.

An estate sale where someone has actually died is a mother lode of treasure even if the choicest items have gone to auction. Heirs often have no appreciation for the real value of Bavarian crystal bowls, Irish linen tablecloths or silver candlesticks - and you hit pay dirt.

DID YOU KNOW?

You can get great prices at the end of the day at an estate sale when the family is burned out and just wants it all over.

The moving 'estate' sale of an affluent family produces valuable castoffs like guestroom TV's, duplicate blenders and food processors, and pristine baby beds and high chairs used only when grandchildren visited at Christmas.

You are absolutely expected to bargain. You get the best prices when you bundle several things and make an offer for the batch. The usual 'get there early rule' can be trumped by the latecomer who does well when the family is tired of strangers, haggling over pennies, and just wants the whole thing to be over with. This is a fruitful climate for making offers that are likely to be accepted.

garage, yard & moving sales

Shop for: Used bicycles, golf clubs, fishing tackle, bookcases, kitchen appliances, clothing, lawn furniture, tools, board games.
Go early and offer a price for multiple items.

You can find a yard sale or garage sale in almost any neighborhood on any weekend. Sometimes advertised in the local classified ads, sometimes posted with handmade signs on a main thoroughfare, these popular money-making weekend projects have been the mainstay of American suburbia for more than 50 years. They stand beside lemonade stands as models of pure capitalism.

Whole neighborhoods can band together and pool their unwanted junk. With a completely random selection of items and quality, these are good places to find a chest of drawers to refinish, an odd set of golf clubs, or a reading light.

The best hunting grounds are moving sales. People let go of perfectly good stuff because they don't want to pay to move it. Look for an older couple who is downsizing and you'll find almost anything – and almost new.

• • • • • • • • • • • • • • • • • • •

DID YOU KNOW?

The best moving sale is when an older couple downsizes or consolidates homes and sells off perfect condition duplicates.

• • • • • • • • • • • • • • • • • • •

You are absolutely expected to bargain. You get the best prices when you bundle several things you want and then make an offer for the batch.

Professional garage sale shoppers are out early. Get there before the good stuff is gone, because it will go fast.

Oven casserole dish
– $4
garage sale

home parties & gold

Shop for: Unique gold pieces
at cost based on weight.
Purpose is to sell, not buy.
Come home with money
instead of spending it.

Most home parties are driven by some sort of multi-level marketing scheme. While eliminating the retailer, MLM introduces so many middle men taking a profit from every sale that real bargains at your neighbor's lingerie party are rare.

The profitable (*for you too!*) and intriguing gold party with guests invited to sell anything they hope is made from the real thing is the golden exception. They come with Ziploc bags, plastic boxes and velvet sacks brimming with gold bangles, vintage rings, old coins, charm bracelets, broken chains, lone earrings and even gold-backed teeth.

Your hostess invites you to her home and a gold trader sets up an assay station. She uses various chemical reagents to test first if the piece is gold, and then which karat – 10k, 14k and 18k the most common. The piece is then weighed and the price calculated based on the weight alone. There is no consideration given for craftsmanship, as all pieces are destined to be smelted. There is no value given either to gemstones. Stones may be removed before weighing, or the gold merchant can guestimate the weight of the piece minus stones.

Payment is immediate, in large bills, and can be quite heady. Cash is always king; there's just nothing else like it. The dealers have fixed rates per weight for each karat class (10k, 14k, 18k), but it might be possible to bargain for a higher price per ounce. It never hurts to ask.

DID YOU KNOW?

Gold party traders give you cash on the spot in crisp $50 and $100 bills.

Gold parties are designed for you to sell your own bits and pieces to the trader. But guests can also buy from each other, or trade. If you use the professional to determine the price, you can buy beautiful pieces from other guests at greatly discounted prices. The trader pays less for the gold than she receives from the purchasing smelter, creating a price point for party gold sales below the wholesale market.

She would prefer you sell the gold to her, rather than you selling to your friends, but is often willing to assist any side

Nancy, happy gold partier
with hundred dollar bills.

sales by setting the price. They want you to be happy. They want to book more parties. Besides, most attendees are more interested in taking home cash than more jewelry.

Expect to dismantle some jewelry to ascertain the correct weight and price. It is not unusual to find a mix of 10-karat and 14-karat gold, or even gold-plate, in one piece. Bracelets with gold charms or watches with gold chains are generally taken apart. A small clear plastic box with gold-backed teeth brought $300 after the teeth had been smashed with a hammer. Macabre perhaps - but who wouldn't rather have money than Great Auntie's teeth in a little box?

It is always your decision to proceed or not – at any time. Individual sales range from $30 to $3000, but can be more - it all depends on what goodies the guests bring. The trader pays the hostess a percentage of the sales. A party of 20, starting at 1:00 and ending by 4:00, netted the hostess $750 - a sweet little afternoon 'work' that was a win-win for everyone.

internet shopping sites

Shop for: Anything, anywhere, at any price.
New merchandise.
Perfect for the catalogue shopper.

There are thousands of sites on the internet selling every kind of merchandise at every price. Google, Yahoo, MSN – all of their homepages have shopping options where a click of the mouse can transport you to a universe of buying opportunities.

The disadvantage in buying online is that you can't feel, touch or smell what you're buying. It's like shopping from a giant catalogue with infinite selection and lots of eye candy. The advantage is that you can shop anytime, day or night. Many sites have generous return policies, some do not. Check carefully before you buy.

If you want daily temptation via the ease of your laptop, the website www.GiltFuse.com offers a lavish array of men's, women's and children's designer label clothing, accessories and jewelry, as well as household items 'on sale' for a limited period of time - usually one day. Sale items are organized according to designer labels.

Billed as a members-only site, you receive $25 credit for inviting a friend to join - so much for exclusivity. Once you are a member, you receive regular email updates about new offerings.

The website is beautifully executed with powerful graphics and top quality photography. It's a real class act and a brilliant way to label shop for new clothes and jewelry at discounts of 50% and greater - without leaving home (or your desk.) Their return policy is strict and unforgiving. The site clearly lays out the parameters; most sales are final. A calendar keeps you informed of upcoming sales.

Go to: **http://www.giltfuse.com** to join.

http://www.giltfuse.com

outlet malls

Shop for: Designer label clothing, shoes, bags. New but sometimes damaged or legal knock off. Buyer be aware!

You have surely shopped at an outlet mall and come home with a designer label bag or suit at an impressive discount. But it could be that you paid too much for something that was made especially to stock the shelves of the hundreds of premium outlet malls scattered across the country and around the world.

It's the marketing strategy of the outlet mall to attract shoppers by offering deep discounts on 'label' goods that are presented as equal in quality to those sold at regular stores.

Let's dispel a couple of illusions. Discounts are often based on a mythical retail price known as the manufacturer's suggested retail price or so-called 'reference price.' They may use an inflated reference price to start their discounts, so the price you pay could be very close to a full price.

Name brand stores in outlet malls not only carry last season's models and damaged or slightly blemished goods, they can actually mix in lower quality items manufactured just to sell in outlet mall stores. You buy a well-known and respected label, but it's not the craftsmanship and quality the label represents - and you think you are getting. In a way, they are selling knock offs of their own designs. As high as 80% of goods sold in some outlet stores are these lower end pieces.

We all want a killer deal on a bag with a label that will impress our friends. Look for sales at any of the department stores that are slashing prices. Better yet, check out secondhand and consignment shops to get the quality that goes with the label - at seriously discounted pricing.

You can always find a deal – anywhere. But be careful that you don't pay too much for a lower quality than you expect. Consumer laws notwithstanding, it's a tad naïve to assume that everything a store says or claims is completely honest and true.

It you like it, buy it. But do it with your eyes wide open.

• • • • • • • • • • • • • • • • • •

DID YOU KNOW?

Some designers manufacture lower quality goods to sell under their labels at outlet malls.

• • • • • • • • • • • • • • • • • •

pawn shops

Shop for: Diamond rings,
Rolex watches, shotguns, cameras
and electric guitars
Deep discounts for the real thing.

If you've decided that you still want the real thing – the diamond or Rolex watch - then the place for you is a pawn shop. Bigger cities mean bigger selection and a wealthy demographic translates into higher quality and more opportunity for great buys.

Pawn shops aren't just the sleazy holes-in-the-wall depicted in the movies. Think location, location, location. Many pawn shops resemble jewelry stores, but with a wider inventory that includes guns, musical instruments and anything else a pawn broker thinks is worth a loan.

When a pawn shop represents a ring as 14k gold with an H, S1, 2-karat, brilliant-cut stone, you can probably count on it. The best pawn shops provide a diamond certificate, also called a grading report, which is a written evaluation performed by a qualified professional using special gemological instruments. Ask for the report before you buy, for your peace of mind and the insurance underwriter.

The pawn shop has loaned money on each item for sale, using it as collateral. They survive because they are good at valuing and savvy about what they buy. They aren't interested in getting stuck with fake after paying for real. But it's still up to you to get every bit of information you need to feel comfortable before you buy. Although the cost will be far below normal retail, it will still be in the hundreds or even thousands of dollars.

• • • • • • • • • • • • • • • • • •

DID YOU KNOW?
There are many legitimate pawn shops which sell excellent quality, fully documented diamonds at 'bargain' prices.

• • • • • • • • • • • • • • • • • •

This is bargain hunting for those who have serious mad money. But if you are truly a smart shopper, it doesn't make a lot of sense to put all your money in one 'real' piece when you can have a jewel box full of excellent knock offs that defy detection except by a gemologist.

• • • • • • • • • • • • • • • • • •

DID YOU KNOW?
Insurance on real diamonds can cost you hundreds of dollars a year?

• • • • • • • • • • • • • • • • • •

Insurance rates are tied to the replacement value of the appraised stone and not to what you paid for it. A large stone can mean several hundred dollars a year to insure. If paying the extra premium is not a big deal, then buy some impressive bling at the pawn shop and enjoy. No doubt about it, it's a very special kind of feeling when your ice is the real thing.

It's a very special feeling when you own the real thing.

Maxferd's of San Francisco
You'll find selection ranging from a couple of hundred dollars to tens of thousands - something for any wallet.

secondhand stores

Shop for: Carefully screened, secondhand clothing in excellent condition.
No-brainer, no effort shopping.

Independently-owned stores or chains like Buffalo Exchange offer secondhand clothing in a boutique environment, complete with sales help, organized displays and sometimes a return policy.

But even secondhand stores can be upscale and charge steep prices for quality used clothing - especially for sought-after labels. You are paying a finder's fee, plus rent and overhead for a boutique that specializes in recycling carefully screened secondhand clothing and accessories. If you've got the money, it's still great value. But if you need to stretch your dollars *really* far, look for the many moderately priced shops with less emphasis on labels and more on solid, ready-to-wear fashion, all available without any 'discovery' work on your part.

Secondhand stores differ from consignment shops where people consign the shop items to sell for them and you can often negotiate the price. A secondhand store buys outright from the seller and then adds a standard mark-up to generate profit, just as any retail shop with new clothing. Prices are seldom negotiable, unless the store is independently-owned. But it never hurts to ask!

You can update your wardrobe with the least effort and during your lunch break. Although it's possible to find even better deals if you search hard elsewhere, you can't beat a good secondhand store for selection and convenience. You still pay far less than you would for new fashion and get higher quality for your money.

Buffalo Exchange is a chain specializing in secondhand fashion, carrying some new merchandise among the used 'recycled' clothing, shoes and accessories. It's as close as you'll get to a 'normal' boutique shopping experience with its customer-friendly services, window displays and tidy racks. Here you find a collection of unique items rather than identical blouses in different sizes.

They will buy your belts, purses, clothes and shoes (*excellent condition only!*), and even trade – hence the name "Exchange." Ask other secondhand stores if they offer the same.

"...where recycling is always in style."*

Their marketing strategy segues nicely with the growing environmentally-correct green awareness. Their website boasts, *"*We offer great fashion finds at low prices at Buffalo Exchange...where recycling is always in style.*" Located mainly in the West, they have a few stores elsewhere. Check out their website for locations and more information.

http://www.buffaloexchange.com

swap meets & flea markets

Shop for: Almost anything
– used or new – occasionally quality.
The most adventurous
of all shopping.

You can find virtually anything at a swap meet, sometimes known as flea markets, after the famous *Marche aux Puces* in Paris. The name *swap* has nothing to do with reality; the only swapping that goes on is the exchange of cash for goods.

Usually a weekend affair, these informal markets are supposedly comprised of common folk coming together in an unstructured environment to sell their wares. You don't meet to 'swap' any more than you buy fleas at a flea market. The origin of swaps and fleas is long lost in time.

Swap meets can be held indoors or outdoors, be comprised of permanent booths, makeshift stalls or the beds of pickup trucks. They may charge a nominal entry fee ($1-$2). In many communities the swap meet is held weekly at the local drive-in movie. The weekend outdoor Swap in North Las Vegas has the feel of a provincial *pueblo mercado* south of the border, but much cleaner, safer and less chaotic.

With the atmosphere of a medieval market, you'll discover an extravagant patchwork of wildly diverse 'stuff' scattered on the ground, piled inside tents, folded neatly on tables, or sorted and hung on racks. From the practical to the sublime, you find literally anything including a 'dollar store' with hidden treasures like an orange silk Carolina Herrera scarf for a buck.

Any size of cooking pot at the Swap.

While antique dealers have a love affair with their collections, it's all about the money at the Swap. Steel yourself. It can be heart wrenching. People sell things that they should not have to sell.

Grandmas display rosaries and collections of figurines in

Hoping to make a buck.

hopes of supplementing their social security checks. A moth-eaten Marine dress blues uniform is forlornly draped across the hood of a beat up Chevy pickup.

An American flag, folded and encased in a glass and wooden commemorative box, complete with three spent shells, is half buried in a rubble of junk from someone's garage. What hero died for his country and his memorial ends up here this Saturday morning?

Bargain-hunting can bring you painfully close to humanity. Dress down, look poor and be kind. Be prepared to meet the economic woes of our times face on. There are many tragic stories, although the vendors won't bother you with them. They aren't looking for charity. They are looking to sell. Here is where you can really make a killing. An angry husband in the midst of a nasty divorce peddles his wife's Saga mink jacket for $30. That's just a ridiculously silly price, but you're happy to accommodate.

Bargain hunting can bring you painfully close to humanity.

New merchandise abounds alongside the secondhand: vacuum cleaners in a well-stocked storefront, fabric housed in a canvas tent, cooking pots - huge copper vats to stainless steel saucepans – on display in a permanent stall. Other vendors are there only one weekend, hoping to make more money than in a neighborhood yard sale. Here you find a single pair of size 9 alligator boots, never worn, for $10. Buy immediately. You may never see this again.

If the prices on new goods seem a little *too* cheap, you can guess that the merchandise is not from someone's attic and not acquired through 'proper' channels. How you deal with questionable sources at the Swap is again between you and your personal Shopping God.

The price you agree on is the total price. No sales tax added here. You will also need cash, as very few vendors are set up to take credit cards. Forget writing a check. This is a kind of black market economy, very lightly regulated.

Sales are 'as is,' although vendors with an inventory of new merchandise may operate like a any retail store or discount outlet with a variety of return policies.

Vacuum cleaners, new and used, for sale at the Swap.

Be prepared to buy when you see it and carry everything you purchase. More commercial swap meets rent shopping carts. Bring a cloth bag and some extra plastic sacks. One time vendors sometimes won't even have plastic bags.

Yes, you see piles of junk you could never use, but the prizes are there, for sure – and at prices beyond bargain – more like a *steal*, which may or may not reflect the means of their procurement.

Swap meets and flea markets are cultural experiences as

The Swap has the best deal in town on tires.

much as places to shop. The more ethnically diverse your community, the more colorful your local Swap or flea market will be.

Besides killer deals on both the exotic and mundane, look for cheap services like massage by the minute, reflexology, and fortune telling alongside the fresh produce stands and food stalls that tempt you with local and ethnic taste treats.

It's not quite as good as traveling to foreign lands, but it's the next best thing - and a whole lot cheaper.

Mangoes, in season, $10 a box.

Need a bit of paint for a small job?
This is the ultimate in recycling.

Birdcages at the Swap.

'Cocos' stand at the swap meet serving fresh coconut milk drinks.

thrift stores, Salvation Army & Goodwill

Shop for: Secondhand jeans, shoes,
Hawaiian shirts,
costume jewelry, household items.
Shopping where your money
goes to good causes.

At one time considered only for the down-and-out, the popularity of thrift stores, and especially Goodwill and Salvation Army, has burgeoned. Middle class suburbanites have discovered that although most of the merchandise is tired and mismatched, the remaining treasures make a periodic look-see more than worthwhile.

A thrift store is a charity with a special tax status; donations qualify for deduction on income tax returns. Churches and women's auxiliaries use them to raise money for their organizations. The Salvation Army is focused on redistribution of goods to the needy. Goodwill is a non-profit set up to train people for a more productive life by employing them in their retail outlets and repair centers. One part of their community outreach mission is to make professional clothes available to the job-seeker who can't afford an interview suit.

Barb equips her Tahoe kitchen from the local thrift stores.

from left to right:
Rice steamer (electric) - $10
Pink dinner plates - $1 ea
Purple Pyrex saucepan - $1
Metal enamel mixing bowl - $4
Corel dinner plates - $1 ea
Set of 4 coffee mugs - $5
Orange china ashtray - $2
Sugar bowl with lid - $1
Wooden bar stools (2) - $15
Padded cushions (2) - $8
Barb's orange knit sheath - $6

Thrift stores are getting more sophisticated in their marketing and in-store sales promotions as the diversity of their merchandise and clientele improves. Goodwill operates Superstores with shopping carts and special 2-hour sales on children's clothing announced over the PA system, with senior days and military discounts. Salvation Army has a special 'Sally' section stocked with higher quality and better condition donations tagged as appealing to their new middle class (*and above!*) shopper.

Charity thrift store
San Luis Obispo CA

You never know what you will find. People donate old and new, torn and perfect. The reasons behind the donation are as varied as the stories of the donators. Some are cleaning out closets, others are moving. They load up the

SUV for a drive to the Goodwill donation station. Others take their more valuable castoffs to a consignment shop, or secondhand store to sell, donating the humdrum to the Thrift. Some take everything to the ladies auxiliary store because they want to contribute to a good cause. The Goodwill or Salvation Army store is often the last dumping ground of yard sale leftovers. One trip and all those discards are out of your life.

The Salvation Army store in Lahaina, Maui has one of the largest selections of Hawaiian shirts and *mu-mus* anywhere, all collected from tourists leaving behind twice-worn hibiscus-patterned *aloha* shirts. We outfitted our family of five in jackets and sweaters for the freezing (*yes!*) sunrise viewing from Mt. Haleakala - for a total cost of $30. At those prices, you just donate back when you leave.

You can always find something
you like for under $10.

Whatever the reason for any donation at any thrift store, you will always find something you like – and often for under $10.

Check out the website **www.thethriftshopper.com** for thrift stores across the U.S. Add your local store if not listed.

travel jewelry

Shop for: Quality knock off 'diamond' rings, bracelets, necklaces and earrings at fraction of cost. Why buy real?

Asians, especially Thais, are making travel or fine jewelry knock offs that are so real looking, they fool anyone except a gemologist. First dubbed 'travel jewelry' for those who wanted to leave the real thing safely at home, this market has evolved quickly to cater to anyone wanting a fine jewelry look for a fraction of the price.

Why pay for the real thing when you can impress without the sticker shock? A 3-karat, yellow, radiant cut diamond faced with two 1-karat, white, trilliant cut stones mounted in white gold would cost you the down payment on a very nice house on the golf course – maybe more. Buy the identical-looking travel ring and you pay $250-$800, depending if it's on sale - and everything is on sale today.

New techniques in bonding gold to metal (*electroplating*) have virtually eliminated the telltale wear of old-fashioned plating, but the most durable still is always the highest quality, even in knock offs. You can find all prices and all levels of craftsmanship. It's not unusual to see a stunning bracelet with a really lousy clasp. If you are after the 'real' look, then buy the highest-end knock off you can find. The little extra you pay is worth it. Why look fake when you can show off something that will fool everyone?

Some of the best quality in knock off jewelry is sold at Landau and Erwin Pearl, among others. They offer classical, fine jewelry styles at slightly inflated prices in stores found in airports, hotels and pricier shopping malls. Look for store locations and some of their selection at:

http://www.landaujewelry.com

http://www.erwinpearl.com

Quality Elegance Wholesale Jewelry manufactures knock offs copied right out of glossy ads in magazines like *Town and Country*. Their selection is varied and imaginative with something for every taste and budget. Prices are phenomenal, far below the retail outlets, and they sell direct through their website: **www.qualityelegance.com**.

Load up a jewelry box full of delightful choices at budget prices for the cost of one real piece. Own a knock off Tiffany choker for less than the cost of insuring one diamond for a year. Your choice of fake over real also means you are not contributing to the 'blood diamond' trade that causes so much pain and suffering by subsidizing vicious wars.

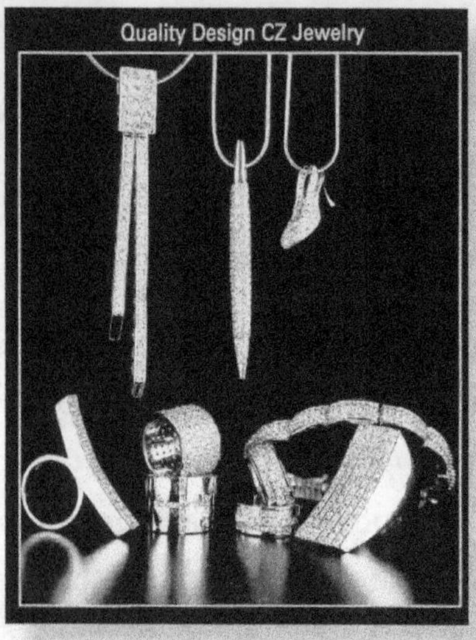

So *why* do you need the real thing?

http://www.landaujewelry.com
http://www.erwinpearl.com
http://qualityelegance.com

vintage clothing shops & websites

Shop for: Quality fabric & cut,
superior craftsmanship in dresses, furs,
hats, gloves, bags and jewelry.
You may pay a premium
- or not.

There are many good books and articles written about vintage clothing shops. As vintage has become more popular, vendors have cashed in on the trend and raised their prices accordingly. That doesn't mean that you can't find beautiful vintage clothing in your price range; it just means that you have to look a little harder to find bargains.

Quality and cost very much depend on the location of the shop and its clientele. Some trendy vintage shops specialize in couture labels and charge hefty finder's fees - reflected in the price tag. The better the condition and the bigger the name on the label, the higher the price to vintage connoisseurs who *really love* clothes and are willing to pay what it costs to own them - sometimes for display only. They regard these creations as fine art - and rightfully so.

If you are looking for truly rare and exquisite vintage fashion, check out the website **www.1stdibs.com.**

Featuring haute couture designers Dior, Versace and Yves Saint Laurent among others, you can expect to pay full value for any of the selection of the very finest in high quality vintage. The site boasts *"the most beautiful things on earth."* Its array of vintage high fashion, furniture and jewelry does not disappoint.

The website **www.thewaywewore.com** focuses exclusively on clothing and promises *"vintage clothing to wear, collect or inspire"* and welcomes you to a *"designer and fashionista's paradise."* Look here not only for vintage but also retro-costumes such as 40's swing dresses, 50's cocktail dresses and poodle skirts, 60's flower child and 70's disco.

http://www.1stdibs.com
http://www.thewaywewore.com

If you are lucky enough to find a small shop with quality items that doesn't cater to movie stars, you can discover rare finds of superb fabric and cut almost non-existent in contemporary clothing even at top prices. You could argue that the quality of some vintage items surpasses today's fashion, no matter the price. There are some real works of art to be found, appreciated and worn.

Look for the best prices on vintage clothing, not in specialized shops, but at antique malls with multiple vendors selling a few items of vintage clothing.

There are some real works of art to be found, appreciated and worn.

Vintage clothing doesn't have to mean you look like you are dressed like someone stepping out of a 50's, 60's or 70's movie. There is certainly nothing wrong with that, if that is the image you want. But if your own taste runs to 21st century, don't rule out updating your vintage finds with small alterations like hem length, removal of shoulder pads and change of buttons that give a classic look rather than a dated one. It is as much about the fabulous fabric and exquisite detailing as the style itself.

DID YOU KNOW?

You can find the best deals on vintage clothing, not in specialized shops, but at antique malls.

Just as in an antique shop, bargains can still be found in a vintage store. If you have the funds, a vintage Balenciaga gown should cost far less than a new one and certainly be just as luxurious in fabric and styling - maybe more so.

Step 11
make it work!

Look for unique opportunities hidden under layers of dirt or disguised by outdated design. These are the real jewels that just need a little TLC to sparkle. Their value and potential went unnoticed because no one had taken the time and effort to really look.

With a minimum of restoration, these diamonds in the rough can be worth 10 or even 100 times more than you pay. But the monetary value is nothing compared to the pride and satisfaction you have in your trophy as it is revealed in all its splendor. The real thrill of the hunt is in discovering beauty no one else saw. You become a co-creator by restoring, re-shaping and renewing.

The real thrill of the hunt is in discovering beauty no one else saw.

If you doubt that great things are lying around in obscure places waiting for your discovery, watch the PBS Antique Road Show to catch a glimpse of the unique and precious stashed away in attics and basements. These are the best pieces, of course, and have been cleaned up for the show. Some of them have languished for years before a curious eye espied them and decided there was beauty and value beneath the dusty veil.

It only takes one unappreciative nephew to place his Aunt's heirlooms before you at a Saturday morning estate sale for you to score big.

The best savings come when you fix it yourself.

vintage clothing & fabric

Beautiful natural fabrics were much more common in the past than today. High quality wool was luxuriant and soft. Silk velvet had a texture and sheen unparalleled by any synthetic. Beadwork sewn in sweatshops in 1950's Hong Kong stays solidly in place. Look for fabric alone - it's so easy to recycle. If there is enough of it, you can create something totally new and vibrant. If you like the fabric and the basic lines of the dress, but think the styling is too dated, learn to tailor or find someone who can.

Obviously the best savings come when you can do it yourself. Not everyone likes sewing, but there are still a few small things you can do to re-invent a superlative hand-knit Italian suit that would cost hundreds in a store, if you could find it.

easy fixes:

Take it in if too big.

Add insert if too tight in the waist but fits hips.

Take out the shoulder pads.

Remove the ruffle.

Take up the hem.

Make it a straight skirt - or an A-line.

Patch small holes.

Change out buttons.

Replace zippers (*drycleaners do this for a small charge*).

Glue loose beads.

Dry-clean.

Hand wash.

Try another belt.

Find a hat.

Dramatize a camel wool suit with a mink collar that you picked up for $25 in the adjacent stall.

You get the idea……

The only limit is your own imagination.

The only limit is your own imagination – let it soar! You create a unique look that updates a 60's evening suit, better than new because the silk brocade is divine, the edging is hand-stitched, and no one skimped fabric on the cut. You turn heads when you enter the room and who would ever guess you re-fashioned this stunning number from a $30 Saturday morning find?

vintage hats

There are some places that just have fabulous collections of hats. It's a specialty for some vendors. They keep an eye out for quality and pass on their finds to you at great prices. Feathered Oscar de la Renta and Chanel are still to be found in wearable condition.

Esperanza examining the merits of a vintage hat. - $20

antique mall

It's easy to glue a loose feather or two to refurbish these gems and voila! - Audrey Hepburn. The netting on vintage hats often needs to be replaced, which is easy enough. Just this simple change freshens and updates. If the brim is out of shape, you can block it by remolding with paper and steaming - or use razor thin wire to re-shape.

bags and purses

There are oodles of secondhand and vintage purses for sale everywhere. Most are in good condition, but look closely at the lining and the clasps. A good shoe repairman can fix a bag in need of a little help, but it must be something you really love to be worth the effort. Unless it's a most unusual piece, insist on excellent condition. Let it go and keep looking. You'll find something better.

DID YOU KNOW?

A good shoe repairman can fix a bag in need of a little help.

jewelry

Hands down, some of the showiest vintage treasures are the marvelous pieces of jewelry showcasing exquisite design and superior craftsmanship - all yours for a song. Most used and vintage jewelry sold is fully functional. Only at a garage sale or swap meet might you find a broken clasp.

Generally the only thing you need to do is clean your piece to bring out its true beauty. Invest in a jeweler's sonicator to bring out the sparkle in most pieces - especially glittering stones from crystals to diamonds. This simple machine, which cleans with sound waves and water, will give almost any piece new life. Years of dust, body oils, cosmetics and creams are removed in minutes.

DID YOU KNOW?

It's easy to clean vintage and estate jewelry to bring out the true beauty.

Sonicator
Rio Grande Ultrasonic Cleaner CD-2800

A word of caution about sonicating and the use of chemicals on vintage jewelry that is painted or glued. The paint or enamel can flake off and the glue can loosen and cause stones to fall out. It's not difficult to re-glue a stone, but paint or enamel cannot be easily repaired, if at all.

Make sure the stones are set with prongs and not glued. If they are glued, use the sonicator with caution and no chemicals, just plain water. If a few stones fall out, simply re-glue.

DID YOU KNOW?

Professionals can restore worn jewelry to its original finish by a chemical plating process that bonds new gold to the old surfaces.

Most sparkly gems, natural and man-made, benefit from a cleaning solution added to the sonicating water. Always sonicate in stages, checking the condition of each piece at 2-3 minute intervals. Some of the shiny colored stones in vintage jewelry have been color-coated on the back side. You don't want to lose that special effect, so go cautiously as you clean.

Precious metals like gold and silver as well as pewter and brass do beautifully with the sonicator and water with a dilution of cleaning agent. If you suspect the piece is merely gold-plated, go cautiously, checking every 2-3 minutes to make sure the plating is not being removed.

• •

DID YOU KNOW?

New techniques in electroplating create knock offs you can treat like the real thing.

• •

Modern pieces are not plated in the same way as vintage jewelry. New techniques in electroplating create knock offs you can treat like the real thing.

You can purchase cleaning solutions at any jewelers or grocery store, but you can make your own from equal parts

A private collection of treasures found 'antiquing.'

liquid dishwashing detergent and ammonia. Remember cleaning solutions are meant to be dissolved in water. A few drops are all you need. Windex, highly diluted in water (*a few drops only*), works wonders on anything sparkly.

A sonicator is not a necessity. Dip the pieces in any manufactured or homemade cleaning solution for a few minutes, then use a soft toothbrush to remove built up dirt and oils. But it's the sonicating machine that delivers the unmistakable professional look. That's why jewelry looks so 'new' when you have it cleaned by a professional.

• • • • • • • • • • • • • • • • • •

DID YOU KNOW?

You can control how 'antique' a piece looks by cleaning it yourself and deciding when to stop.

• • • • • • • • • • • • • • • • • •

Certain pieces will need a lot of cleaning; you may sonicate for 20 minutes or more the first time. Imagine the years of gunk and buildup. One of the advantages of doing your own cleaning is that you can decide when to stop. How 'antique' a look do you want?

Once the jewelry is cleaned to the look that you want, it takes only an occasional refresher of 2-4 minutes to bring it to full sparkle. Keep a sonicator on your bathroom vanity and drop your pieces in before you go out.

Furniture

Consignment shops are among the best places to find used furniture needing minor repair. Imagine a sturdy black lacquer 5'x40" rectangular dining table with two leaves for an amazing $98 at Colleen's in Henderson, NV. A quick touch up with a black Sharpie and what a buy!

Dining room table with two leaves
- $98 - consignment shop
Scratches touched up with black Sharpie.
Candlesticks - $2.50
Salvation Army

You *can* do most simple repairs. Some kind of fine-tuning is almost always necessary when you buy secondhand furniture – whether at Goodwill, Salvation Army, thrift stores, swap meets or garage sales. Be ready to use a screwdriver to tighten loose screws and a paintbrush, Sharpie or wood repair crayons to take care of scratches and nicks. Any hardware store should have an array of different colored crayons designed to camouflage flaws in a variety of woods.

You can't be a perfectionist. Don' be too fanatical. Think gestalt. Who looks that closely anyway? If you can't see it from three feet, it's not there.

Think gestalt. If you can't see it from 3 feet, it isn't there.

ceramic pot - $30 - collectibles shop
Generously marred with scratches and nicks touched up with black Sharpie - all non-existent when applying the 3 foot-rule.

Frame with beveled mirror
- $35
antique mall
Touched up with gold paint from Michael's.

your best friend is a good oil. Use simple olive oil to get lustrous results. Vegetable oils are best on picture frames and items with no direct human contact because they don't absorb quickly and can be smudgy. Be sparing in your use of all oils. Put a small amount on a clean rag and apply gently to the surface. Avoid pouring oil directly on the surface. It takes longer to polish with the oil on a cloth, but you get much better results. Cotton rags are best. Buy them in packets or better yet recycle men's cotton undershirts; they are soft and absorbent. Throw them into the washing machine with hot water, soap and bleach to last forever.

re-upholstering solves most problems. If you are ambitious and willing to invest more time and money, there are great buys in chairs and sofas needing fresh upholstery. This can be expensive, however, unless you do it yourself. If you have the budget to revamp a piece with good 'bones,' select a fabric and get a professional to do the work. It will be well worth it. There is no faster way to update than re-upholstering.

DID YOU KNOW?

All you need to re-upholster the seat of a dining chair is a square piece of fabric, a screwdriver and a staple gun.

You can re-upholster or re-cover many projects yourself. Although re-upholstering a sofa or chair requires special skill, there are many simple solutions. Slipcovers can do marvels for tatty but comfortable sofas. Re-covering the seats of chairs is often as easy as removing the seat plate (*screwdriver*), taking off the old cloth (*usually stapled or nailed on*), wrapping the wooden plate in new fabric squares, re-stapling, and re-screwing the covered plate to the chair frame. Victorian cherry side chairs are chic and updated with zebra striped canvas or leopard velour. You choose the fabric - no sewing required.

dressers and chests are an easy and creative facelift. Changing out drawer and cabinet knobs is one of the fastest and cheapest ways to update dressers and chests. It's easy to sand old paint or varnish and re-treat the wood with one of the many stain products on the market. Most any painting technique you use on walls can be used on furniture. Try experimenting with painting geometric patterns or floral trim.

DID YOU KNOW?

Updating an old dresser is as easy as replacing the knobs. You can experiment with any wall finishing techniques sold in the paint department.

Fabric - $5 Regency-style sconce curtain rod holders - $6 ea
fabric store - close-out sale
No sewing. Approx. 30 minutes for hand-pleating and hanging.

It's incredibly therapeutic to work with your hands. The mind moves at a calmer pace when the hands are busy, especially if the right brain is creating at the same time.

> The mind moves at a calmer pace when the hands are busy.

art, artifacts, objets d'art, tsatske

This is the genre most associated with antique stores and estate and garage sales. Here is prime hunting ground for large and small, rare and unusual objects in all price ranges and in all conditions. It is completely up to you how 'perfectionist' you want to be and what level of defect you can accept if the price is right.

If you fall in love with a green glass decanter that resembles a Baghdad minaret and discover a small chip in the stopper, buy it for yourself and live with the blemish – especially when it only cost you $12!

Green glass decanter (small chip in stopper) - $12

antique shop

Remember to think gestalt and use the 3 foot rule. With crystal and glass, you either buy perfect or learn to live with small imperfections - there is no homemade fix for chipped edges. Grinding small nicks from the rims of crystal goblets and bowls is still done in Europe, but is not a growth industry here in the U.S. New Englanders and Southerners have more respect for history, so you might get lucky there.

Visit the Swap or antique mall if you want surprise and adventure.

Any true collectible that is broken, scratched or otherwise flawed is greatly reduced in value. Collectors are generally interested in excellent condition only. Go to eBay if you want perfection and ease in collecting. Visit the Swap or antique mall if you want surprise and adventure.

frames and mirrors

The best finds are usually just dusty, dirty and generally lacking TLC. You can find beautiful picture frames and mirrors that glow after oiling and polishing. Use an index finger with an olive oil-soaked cotton cloth to gently rub the surface, removing dirt or even mold. Oil was the primary cleaning agent in ancient times, the only choice besides water and sand in the millennia before soap.

• • • • • • • • • • • • • • • • • •

DID YOU KNOW?

Olive oil is one of the safest cleaners for old wood and painted frames. Oil, sand and water were the only cleaning options for thousands of years.

• • • • • • • • • • • • • • • • • •

Paint wooden and metal frames if you like the basic bones but not the finish. A can of spray paint is the best technique for an even color or a base. You are limited only by your own fantasy – or willingness and ability to copy.

There are two types of 'gold' or gilt frames. The most common are those that have simply been painted with gold paint. These you can gently clean with oil. The more expensive and precious gold frames are covered in actual *gold leaf*, the thinnest of thin sheets of real gold hammered (*ever so delicately!*) onto the wooden frame. A typical design includes an elaborate geometric or floral/ leaf pattern carved into the wood. A skilled craftsman is required to apply (and repair) the gold leaf.

Gold prices as they are, these frames are rarer and more expensive. Keep an eye out for good buys from unsuspecting vendors who don't know the difference, and conversely, don't pay for gold leaf when it's only paint. The photo on the facing page shows the difference.

Detail of frame with both
gold leaf (bottom) and gold paint (top).

• • • • • • • • • • • • • • • • • • •

DID YOU KNOW?

There are two types of gold frames used for paintings and mirrors. Gold-painted wood is inexpensive and common, while gold leaf is more rare, extremely delicate and made from real gold.

• • • • • • • • • • • • • • • • • • •

Do not attempt to clean gold leaf. The gold will flake off. Some flaking is inevitable, especially when the frame is moved. Careful handling is required at all times to preserve the work.

Old mirrors have a certain charm with their slightly muddied and cracked surfaces. You may not want that level of 'antique' look, but are attracted to the design of the frame. Point out the deficiencies of the mirror, bargain for the best price, restore the frame as needed, and purchase new mirror at your local glass shop. The best mirrors are beveled on the edges, which gives them an upscale look. You can purchase beveled mirrors, but usually only in standard shapes and sizes. A 90-year-old oval frame will require a custom beveled mirror - not cheap. A sheet of ordinary mirror, cut to size, costs much much less. If the frame is beautiful, few will notice the lack of bevel.

DID YOU KNOW?

You can seriously damage artwork or gold leaf by cleaning without proper skill or tools.

oil paintings, watercolors, drawings

Restoring oil paintings or watercolor art is absolutely a job for a professional. Do not attempt to restore any original art work, no matter the media. Include lithographs and photographs in this category. You can lightly dust the canvas and polish the frame, but you can wreck extensive damage if you attempt to clean brushwork, charcoal, pastels or other media without proper tools and training.

Unframed painting of Venetian scene
-$75
antique mall

Inlaid table-$1000
White quartz geode - $500
antique mall

Final thoughts

happy shopping!

Creating and writing this book has been my personal Zen odyssey. What could be more fun than shopping for bargains and then sharing my stories?

I have met wonderful people who already 'get it.' I've had rousing discussions about *"shopping is to women what sex is to men."* I have talked with women who claim they're not interested in shopping. Maybe they believe it themselves. It might be true. I have heard of men who aren't interested in sex, although I have personally never met any.

What's living rich? Of course it's important to look our best and surround ourselves with beauty and quality. But living rich is much more than owning beautiful things. It's living life to the fullest. Be open to change and possibility; look for fun and adventure. Be ready to act when the Universe extends a helping hand.

Your life is an intricate web of emotional experiences. You will feel more powerful with each killer deal and new trophy. More self-confident, your energy will manifest a joyous and fulfilling life, one in touch with the real you and your true place in the ebb and flow of the Universe.

Thank you for coming this far with me on the journey. Remember to live rich, look good and be happy.

See you at the Swap!

Mystic Pot
- $3

Goodwill

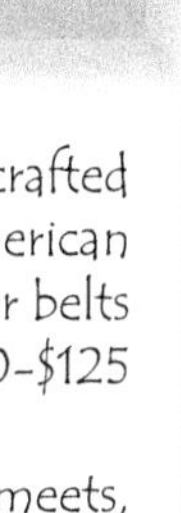

vintage hand-crafted
Native American
silver belts
$50-$125

swap meets,
garage sales,
estate sales

Golf clubs and balls
- $10 total - swap meet

Philosophy in Pull Quotes

Philosophy in Pull quotes

Philosophy in Pull quotes

index

A

B

C

L

M

N

O

P

Q

R

Serape - wool - used as wall hanging
$10 - thrift store

notes

Antiques at the Market
6665 S. Eastern Ave, Las Vegas NV 89119

Children's Cabinet Thrift Store
790 Northwood Blvd, Incline Village, NV 89451
www.cciv.org

Colleen's Classic Consignment
1235 W. Warm Springs Rd, Henderson NV 89014
3071 N. Rainbow Blvd, Las Vegas NV 89108
www.colleenconsign.com

East End Hospice Thrift
481 Riverhead Rd, Westhampton Beach, NY 11978
www.eeh.org

Hospice Partners Hope Chest
445 Higuera St, San Luis Obispo, CA 93401
www.hospicepartners.org

Loehmann's
222 Sutter St, San Francisco, CA 94108

Maxferd Jewelry & Loan
201 Kearny St, San Francisco, CA 94108

Old Mission School Thrift Store
2460 Broad St, San Luis Obispo, CA 93401

The Nest
800 Palm St, San Luis Obispo, CA 93401
www.thenestinslo.com

Seaside Collectibles
1327 Shell Beach Rd, Shell Beach, CA 93449

References

1. "Women think shopping, men think about sex."
By Andy Bloxham @ http://www.telegraph.co.uk/

2. "Women think about shopping as much as men think about sex."
By David Wilkes @ http://www.dailymail.co.uk/femail

About the author

Born in Kansas City, Sandra Gore Nielsen is a baby boomer who escaped the Plains on a one way ticket to Iceland and beyond to explore the world while her friends were partying at college.

She returned to the United States after twenty-five years in Europe, Africa, Central America and the Middle East, with a Danish husband, an art degree and speaking five languages.

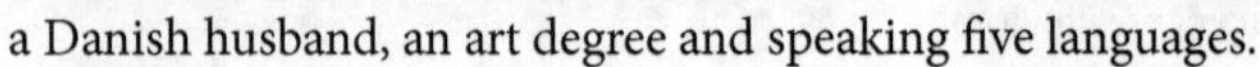

After her traveling era came family, business and politics. She and her husband raised a daughter and son in a beach house in Central Coast California, starting up and managing a successful scientific company. Sandra was a political activist and environmentalist and served as an elected official and Planning Commissioner.

Her writing era began in Las Vegas with the creation of www.sandraoffthestrip.com, a magazine blog dedicated to the adventures of an eclectic mind. "Sex and the Zen of Shopping" is her first self help, how to manual. Sandra contributed the real life fairy tale "A True Love Story" to the anthology "Life Choices - Navigating Difficult Paths" published by Turning Point International.

Sandra is slowly compiling a cookbook of her own recipes as well as the best from talented friends around the globe. Her next book, a memoir of her travel adventures, includes a six month hitchhike journey across the Sahara.

Thank you

Writing a book takes the support of friends and family. I give special thanks to Esperanza Montelongo for my inspiration, April Lynch for professional guidance, Barbara Johnston for bravery as First Reader, Paulette and Leo Anderson for spiritual guidance, Patricia Derrick for vision, Sylvia Muscia for her savvy, Cheryl Weiss for discerning critique, Ann Calhoun for post print energy, David and Carol Georgi for believing in me, and Peg Pinard for always being my friend. Extra thanks go to Jesper, Alexia and Rex for saving me from drowning in technology over my head.

Colophon

Sandra Gore Nielsen is author, layout designer, cover artist, and photographer for "Sex and the Zen of Shopping."

Alexia Nielsen assisted with the fine-tuning of photographs and cover fonts using Adobe Photoshop.

Rex Nielsen assisted with the cover design in Adobe Photoshop.

Jesper Nielsen assisted in everything, including the technical trials and tribulations of Adobe InDesign CS4 and the intricacies of publishing.

Barbara Johnston assisted as trusted First Reader.

Manuscript preparation and design: Adobe InDesign CS4.
Photo treatment and cover design: Adobe Photoshop.
Cameras: Nikon Coolpix and Leica Digilux II.

Fonts:
Chapter Headers: Cheri.
Script: festus!
Captions: Tempus Sans ITC.
Body text: Minion Pro.
Index: Perpetua.
Cover: cheri liney, Cheri, festus!, Estrangelo Edessa, Candara

Tajine Publishing
2550 E Desert Inn Rd #443 Las Vegas, NV 89121

Discussion Points

Is she crazy or what?

1. Do all women truly love to shop? How does shopping make you feel? Do you look forward to it? Is it an adventure, release, or obligation? Do you enjoy showing off new purchases?

2. Do you tell yourself you don't like to shop because you are disciplining yourself not to spend money?

3. Is it irresponsible to encourage women to shop? Isn't our society too materialistic? Will this book help or hurt women with a shopping addiction? Can a shopaholic learn to be a "smart" shopper?

4. How do you measure your self-worth? Do you associate bargain or secondhand shopping with being poor, not good enough, or promoting a false image?

5. Would you wear a secondhand dress to a graduation party or wedding? Would it depend on whether you bought it at a vintage store or a yard sale?

6. Would you buy something at a swap meet, flea market or garage sale that you suspect is stolen?

7. How does secondhand shopping help the environment? Is it a way to shop "green?"

8. Are you more comfortable bargaining in some situations than others? Do you enjoy beating down the price or would you rather just pay and be done with it?

10. Would you ever go to a flea market, swap meet or yard sale by yourself? Would you go with a friend?

11. Do foreign languages, strange neighborhoods and different looking people intrigue or intimidate you?

12. Can you give up your credit cards and go cash-only?

13. Do you shop with a list and only buy what's on it, or do you also look around and see what catches your eye?

14. Do you have faith in the Universe or some kind of divine providence? Is there a plan? Is there anyone or anything looking out for you?

15. Is there any correlation between shopping and sex? Are women as interested in shopping as men are in sex?

16. Why don't men like to shop? Or do they?

www.ingramcontent.com/pod-product-compliance
Lightning Source LLC
LaVergne TN
LVHW020719110826
845149LV00012B/2335
9780984279913